FDR ON HIS HOUSEBOAT

Also by Karen Chase

KAZIMIERZ SQUARE
(poetry)

LAND OF STONE
BREAKING SILENCE THROUGH POETRY

BEAR
(poetry)

JAMALI-KAMALI
A TALE OF PASSION IN MUGHAL INDIA
(poetry)

POLIO BOULEVARD
A MEMOIR

FDR ON HIS HOUSEBOAT

The *Larooco* Log, 1924–1926

EDITED AND ANNOTATED BY

KAREN CHASE

excelsior editions

State University of New York Press
Albany, New York

Front cover: "FDR swimming in a Warm Springs, GA pool," portion of watercolor painting by Louis Howe, and photo of FDR's houseboat. © FDR Presidential Library & Museum.

Back cover images: Portion of watercolor painting by Louis Howe. © FDR Presidential Library & Museum.

Author photo: Courtesy of Ogden Gigli.

Published by State University of New York Press, Albany

© 2016 Karen Chase (www.karenchase.com)

Printed in the United States of America

Excelsior Editions is an imprint of State University of New York Press

For information, contact State University of New York Press, Albany, NY
www.sunypress.edu

Production, Jenn Bennett
Marketing, Fran Keneston

Library of Congress Cataloging-in-Publication Data

Names: Chase, Karen, editor.
Title: FDR on his houseboat, 1924–1926 : the Larooco log / edited and annotated by Karen Chase.
Other titles: Franklin Delano Roosevelt on his houseboat, 1924–1926 | Larooco log
Description: Albany : State University of New York Press, [2016] | Series: Excelsior editions | Includes bibliographical references and index.
Identifiers: LCCN 2016005985 (print) | LCCN 2016008066 (ebook) | ISBN 9781438462271 (hardcover : alk. paper) | ISBN 9781438462295 (e-book)
Subjects: LCSH: Roosevelt, Franklin D. (Franklin Delano), 1882–1945—Travel—Florida. | Larooco (Boat) | Houseboats—Florida—History. | Logbooks—United States—20th century. | Boat living—Florida. | Florida Keys (Fla.)—Description and travel. | Roosevelt, Franklin D. (Franklin Delano), 1882–1945—Health. | Poliomyelitis—Patients—United States—Biography. | Presidents—United States—Biography.
Classification: LCC E807 .F342 2016 (print) | LCC E807 (ebook) | DDC 973.917092—dc23
LC record available at http://lccn.loc.gov/2016005985

10 9 8 7 6 5 4 3 2 1

As the past rolls into the future, here's to you—

Ruby Chase

Solomon Chase

Quill Chase-Daniel

CONTENTS

ACKNOWLEDGMENTS

Many thanks to many people.

Thanks to all of you at the Franklin D. Roosevelt Presidential Library and Museum in Hyde Park, New York. You radiate a generosity of spirit reminiscent of FDR. Robert Clark, chief archivist, your ongoing gusto was heartening. Thank you for allowing me to examine a document retired from public view, the original *Larooco* log in its old black three-ring binder. *Das Ding an sich*—there is no muse like the thing itself. And thanks to Sarah Malcolm, the archivist who spent hours skillfully scanning the complete log for the facsimile section of this book.

In the fall of 2013, as visiting writer at the FDR Homestead, I worked on the log in the Stone Cottage at Val-Kill, not yet restored. Early each morning, Francesca Macsali-Urbin, a ranger from the National Park Service, would de-alarm the house, unlock the door, and let me in. What a way to start the cold day—hearing Francesca's hometown Roosevelt stories, then being surrounded by the invisible presence of Franklin and Eleanor. Thank you, Francesca.

Later that year, I was a resident writer at Bascom Lodge on top of Mount Greylock, the tallest peak in Massachusetts. Bascom Lodge was built by FDR's Civilian Conservation Corps, which made it a fertile place to work on this book. Peter Dudek, a wonderful sculptor dedicated to improving other artists' lives, thank you for making this residency possible.

To Didi Goldenhar and Jeffrey Harrison, thank you my dear poets, for reading early drafts of this book and sharing your thoughts and especially your concerns. Your critical input was essential.

To Londa Weisman, who for three years lived on the much-loved Baltic schooner *Sofia*, thanks for your early zest for this nautical project after you read a rough first draft.

To Victoria Wright, the expert transcriber of the handwritten log entries by people other than FDR, thanks for your exacting work.

To sea captain Skip Richheimer, thanks for showing me your nautical maps of the Florida Keys so I could track the exact route FDR took each winter, and thanks for setting me straight about how to use nautical terms when describing the houseboat.

To the people of SUNY Press, you are a blessing. Enormous thanks to you all: Amanda Lane-Camilli, who shepherded this project through many stages with excitement, competence, and dedication; Jessica Kirschner, who created beautiful multicolored spreadsheets to make sense of permissions and matters of resolution for all the images that appear in this book; and Donna Dixon, who doggedly searched for resources to help with the digitization of the log.

Thanks to Jenn Bennett, Production Editor Supreme, for her much-needed flexibility and inventiveness, and to Fran Keneston for her skill and spirit as she carries these pages into the world.

Thanks to my literary agent, Jonathan Matson, who unfailingly guides me toward the most constructive route for taking new work into the world.

To Joy Johannessen, my editor, thank you. Your questioning, originality, grasp of the writer's intent, and organizing skill merge at such a high level that I have to wonder whether you're really Maxwell Perkins reincarnated. This book would not exist without your gifts.

Both my parents loved Franklin Delano Roosevelt, so books about him were always flowing through our house; thanks to the memory of Lil and Zenas Block for first introducing me to the man. To my sons, David Chase and Matthew Chase-Daniel, thanks for naming your gerbils Eleanor and Franklin when you were boys—familiarity with the Roosevelts passed down through the generations. Thanks to Quill Chase-Daniel, my grandson, who sat in my office one long afternoon, plying me with questions about FDR and the log, then offering ideas about how to present it, a conversation so alive that it spurred me on.

Thanks to Paul Graubard. You read draft after draft of this book, sharing your focused insights, but there is no thanks enough, husband, for all the times I said to you, "I just need some hot food tonight," and you always came through.

My greatest thanks go to the memory of Franklin Roosevelt.

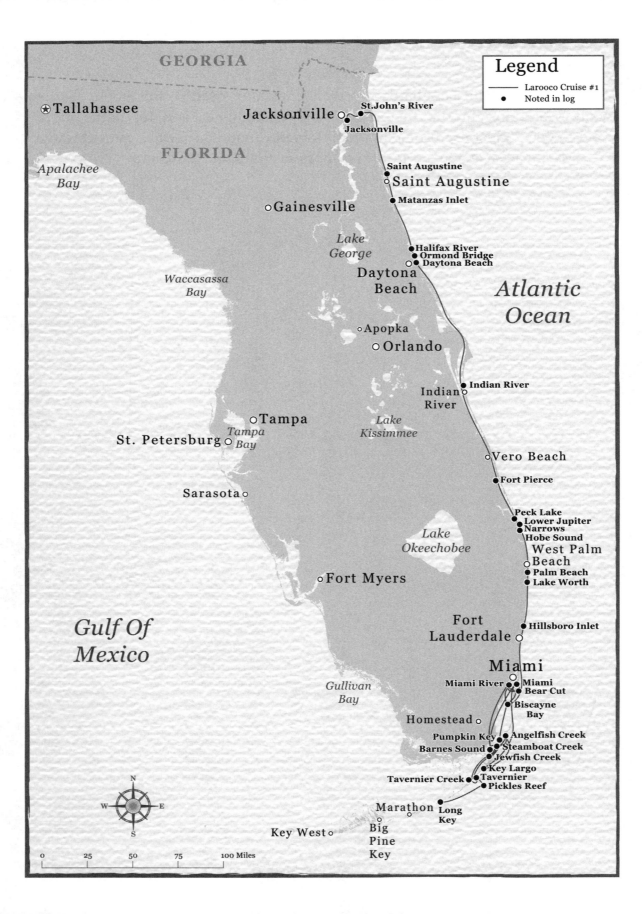

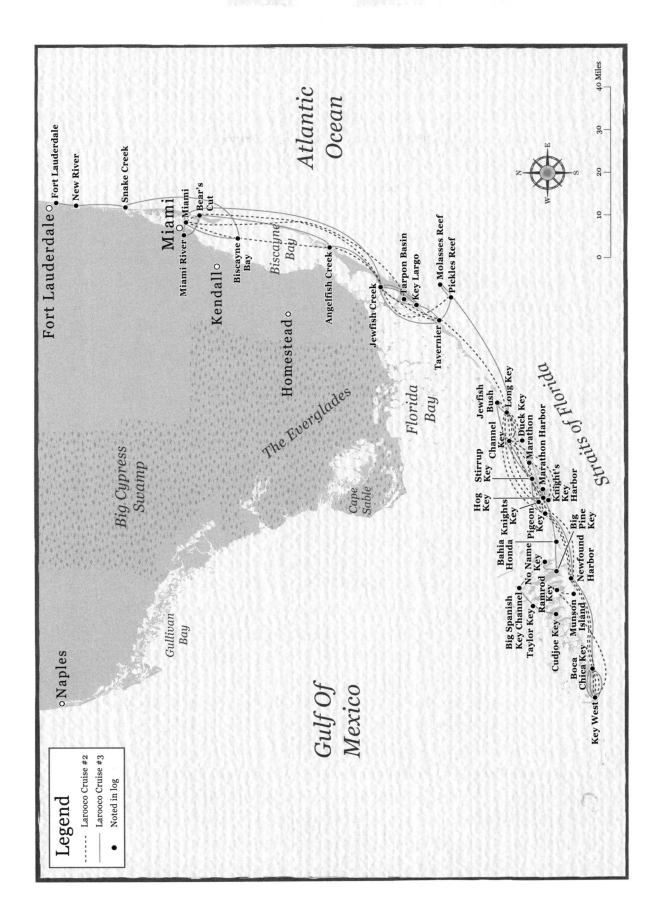

INTRODUCTION

During the Roaring Twenties, a politically ambitious young man who had been crippled by polio bought a houseboat so he could cruise the warm waters of the Florida Keys and try to cure his damaged legs. When Franklin Delano Roosevelt was stricken with the disease in 1921, he withdrew from public life. He spent three winters aboard his houseboat, from 1924 to 1926. While on the boat, he kept a log in longhand in a three-ring binder, writing in it almost every day. Sometimes he used black ink, sometimes turquoise, pages full of playfulness.

> Grog in midst of glorious sunset
> which was almost as poetic in coloring
> as Frances' and Missy's nighties

So he documented one jolly evening. Or reporting on a broken motor:

> Miami Engine doctor at work
> Patient may respond to heroic treatment

A few years ago, I was working on a book about my girlhood polio, a book in which Franklin Delano Roosevelt looms large. Piled on the floor near my desk were four fat navy tomes of his letters. His son Elliott had edited these volumes of his father's personal correspondence in 1949, four years after Roosevelt's death during his fourth term as president. Having FDR's words near me was inspiring and comforting. One day, I picked up one of the books and began trolling around. Buried amidst the letters, I stumbled on Roosevelt's nautical log. His words were captivating. I loved his humor and language—even the repetitive details—and wanted other readers to fall under his spell too. Thus this book.

Roosevelt had always loved boats and water. When he was five, in his first letter to his mother, he enclosed his drawing of sailboats.

One night in August 1921, thirty-four years after he mailed that letter—after he boated, after he fought a forest fire and swam with his children in the Bay of Fundy—he was struck by polio. Roosevelt never walked again.

On August 28, the *New York Times* found it newsworthy to report his illness, though not its exact nature and seriousness.

Franklin D. Roosevelt Better

Franklin D. Roosevelt, former Assistant Secretary of the United States Navy, who had been seriously ill at his Summer home at Campobello, N.B. is recovering slowly. He caught a heavy cold and was threatened with pneumonia. Mrs. Roosevelt and their children are with him.

From then on, FDR tried treatment after treatment in his quest to walk again. Two years later, filled with hopes of healing, he rented a houseboat called the *Weona* and spent a month and a half in the Florida waters, fishing, relaxing, and entertaining guests. From the boat, he wrote his mother, Sara, "This warmth and exercise is doing lots of good," and said his visiting guests "are great fun to have on board in this somewhat negligee existence. All wander around in pyjamas, nighties and bathing suits!"[1]

For FDR's health, his wife, Eleanor, felt compelled to visit the boat, but she disliked the blithe atmosphere. "I tried fishing but had no skill and no luck, when we anchored at night and the wind blew, it all seemed eerie and menacing to me."[2] She left the *Weona* after a few days.

In the summer of 1923, Roosevelt traveled from his home in New York to vacation with Louis Howe, his close political adviser, at Howe's cottage on Horseneck Beach in Massachusetts. Missy LeHand, FDR's assistant, stayed there too, taking care of correspondence. At the beach, Roosevelt tried out new regimens for his legs, working with a well-known neurologist, Dr. William McDonald, who had developed a strenuous course of treatment. FDR jokingly said that if he ever became president, the doctor would be the first visitor to the White House. Occasionally when Howe brought him breakfast, he said, "This is to make you strong. I will see that you become President of the United States."[3]

Sometimes Roosevelt went to the dunes in an old bathing suit, found a secluded spot, and crawled on his hands and knees over the hot sand until he was worn out. Back at the cottage, Howe would fix drinks for the two of them. Picture FDR sipping a martini and discussing politics, having just crawled across the beach. He didn't mind crawling because he could do that himself. What he hated was for others to have to carry him from place to place.

One day that summer, his old college friend John Lawrence stopped by the Howe cottage for a visit. He and his wife had been guests on the *Weona* the winter before. There at Horseneck Beach, the men hatched a plan to buy a houseboat of their own for the coming winter months.

FDR began the search. "What I am looking for is a boat that is fairly low in the water so that I can easily drop overboard and crawl back on deck."[4] In the fall, he found "a real bargain" on Long Island in New York. He wrote to Lawrence, "The owner is apparently up against it financially, and must sell quick!"[5]

The two bought the houseboat, named *Roamer*, for $3,750. Her length overall was 71 feet. She was 19 feet in the beam and drew 3.6 feet. Her hull was about 15 years old and was planked with cypress. She had two 35-horsepower engines.

About renaming the boat, FDR wrote to Lawrence, "It has been suggested that we call her the 'Larose' or the 'Rosela', both of which are euphonious and illustrate the new partnership of Lawrence, Roosevelt and Co."[6] Lawrence replied, "How would you like LAROOCO (Lawrence Roosevelt Co.). The double O and seven letters have usually been typical of good luck in yachts."[7] And so the *Roamer* became the *Larooco*.

As the men prepared for their time on the boat, FDR sent Lawrence a list of who should contribute what.[8]

```
                    MEMORANDUM
                J.S.L.  &   F.D.R.


    1.  To be attended to by J.S.L.

            Purchase & have shipped to F.D.R.,
            49 E. 65th St., N.Y. so as to arrive
            prior to November 8th:

            Cotton sheets - 48 single for cabin ($2 each)
                            15   "     "   crew  ($1.50 ")

            Pillow cases to cover 20" x 28" pillows -
                            36 for cabin (50¢ each)
                            15 for crew  (36¢   " )

            Towels - 108 face towels @ 20¢
                      48 bath   "    @ 50¢
                      50 yards dish toweling.

            Cretonne - 1 roll for curtains & sofa pillows

            Eastern Yacht club private signal - absent
            pennant & any old yacht ensign.
            (ABOVE PRICES ARE MACY'S)

    2.  To be attended to by F.D.R.

            Silver ware - nickel plated knives, forks
                          & spoons - steel knives carving
                          set -

            Blankets - 12 pair army blankets.

            Bed Pillows - 12 for cabin
                           5 for crew
                          12 sofa pillows

            Crockery  - complete for cabin
            Glassware -    "      "    "

            Beds - 2 white enamel 7' x 3'
                   1 bed solid construction 7' x 2½'

            Mattress - 2 for 7' x 2½' bed
```

Missy LeHand, becoming more and more indispensable, was the hostess on the *Larooco*. She had become FDR's private secretary the year before he got polio. A capable, tall, dark-haired, blue-eyed twenty-two-year-old, she was game for fun. At the head of the crew were Robert and Dora Morris, an older married couple from Connecticut, who were paid $125 per month. Captain Morris sailed the boat, and Mrs. Morris cooked and did the housekeeping. The young mechanic George Dyer tried his best to keep the feeble engines running, as did Myles McNichols, known as Mac. Leroy Jones, FDR's black valet, woke him each morning, bathed him, and dressed him.

Roosevelt had the boat sailed from Long Island to the Florida Keys. From the start, it was unreliable. He reported to Lawrence:

Dear John:

The LAROOCO has last been heard from at Bordentown, N.J.,—i.e. where the Raritan Canal comes out into the Delaware, engines apparently working all right, but the steering cable to the rudder broke twice and Captain Morris had to get a brand new cable as the old one was rotting out. . . . (SHE IS LEAKING!)[9]

For three winters, FDR lived on the *Larooco*, fishing and swimming and sunbathing, entertaining friends, drinking and playing games, but most of all tending to his body so that he might walk again. About heading south to find a cure, he explained to one of his doctors:

You doctors have sure got imaginations! Have any of your people thought of distilling the remains of King Tut-ankh-amen? The serum might put new life into some of our mutual friends. In the meantime, I am going to Florida to let nature take its course—nothing like Old Mother Nature, anyway![10]

Roosevelt had been assistant secretary of the navy under Woodrow Wilson and had run unsuccessfully for vice-president in 1920. In 1921, before he got sick, he became vice-president of the New York office of the Fidelity and Deposit

Company of Maryland, an insurance firm. Post-polio, in the fall of 1924, FDR and Basil O'Connor, a lawyer who had given him legal advice in the early 1920s, opened a law practice in New York City. Although FDR was active—he knew no other way—these years were the most politically withdrawn time of his life. When he was approached to reenter politics, he vowed that when he could walk without crutches, he would.

During this period, the Roosevelts' marriage was shifting. When FDR contracted polio, Eleanor ignored their estrangement, which had come about three years earlier when she learned of her husband's affair with her social secretary, Lucy Mercer. At that time, she offered him a divorce, which he refused, promising not to see Mercer again, but from then on, they never shared a bedroom. When he got sick, she chose to nurse him with undivided devotion, tending to all of his most basic needs.

Both Franklin and Eleanor were driven and passionate. As he withdrew to Florida in hopes of healing himself with warmth and water, she overcame her shyness and turned herself into a public figure, ostensibly to keep the Roosevelt name alive.

The year after FDR bought the houseboat, he helped build a separate home for Eleanor and two of her friends, a couple she met when the three worked for the Women's Division of the New York State Democratic Committee. Nancy Cook was a curly-haired, irreverent, dynamic woman in her thirties, and Marion Dickerman, seven years her junior, was an educator.

One summer day, Franklin and the three women were picnicking by the Fall Kill Creek, two miles from the main Roosevelt house in Hyde Park, New York. The women began to worry aloud that FDR's mother would be closing the house up for the winter and they wouldn't have a place to visit until the following spring.

> "But aren't you girls silly?" said Franklin, "This isn't mother's land. I bought this acreage myself. . . . Why shouldn't you three have a cottage here of your own, so you could come and go as you please?"[11]

So began the building project of the "honeymoon cottage" as FDR called it, which he supervised hands-on. He wrote to his daughter Anna, on July 20, 1925:

I have been awfully busy with Mr. Clinton getting prices on lumber, stone work, plumbing, etc. and yesterday telegraphed a bid to Mother and Nan and Marion on behalf of Clinton and Roosevelt, which, if they take, will save them over $4,000! Your Pa is some little contractor![12]

Both husband and wife created cozy, casual, independent living arrangements for themselves. As Eleanor was settling in to the new cottage with Nancy and Marion, FDR was taking up winter residency on the *Larooco* with Missy. Interestingly, Eleanor was close to Missy; she bought her clothes and treated her like a core family member. And FDR was close to Nancy and Marion; he inscribed an old children's book for Marion, *Little Marion's Pilgrimage*:

For My Little Pilgrim, whose Progress is always Upward and Onward, to the Things of Beauty and the Thoughts of Love, and of Light, from her affectionate Uncle Franklin. On the occasion of the opening of the Love Nest on the Val Kill.
January 1,1926.[13]

Although Franklin and Eleanor spent little time together, they remained in constant communication, always aware of each other's doings. While FDR was trying to come to terms both physically and psychologically with his being crippled, Eleanor was carving out an independent private and public course in navigating the world. They found a way to be apart and together that appeared to suit them both. One can only guess how large the toll of hurt.

Missy reported that often, in spite of the general jolly mood on the boat, "It was noon before he could pull himself out of depression and greet his guests wearing his lighthearted façade."[14] Eleanor made a few short visits to the houseboat and found it distasteful. Many friends came and went, as did two of the older Roosevelt children, James and Elliott, pictured on the next page with the family on Campobello Island the summer before FDR was taken ill.

After FDR's first winter on the houseboat, he was introduced to Warm Springs, a Georgia spa town. After the third winter, he was ready to say goodbye to the boat and plunge into the Warm Springs waters, which he felt were more likely to heal his legs. "The water put me where I am, and the water has to put

me back,"[15] he said. Here his focus widened as he founded a rehabilitation center, working to heal not only his own stricken body but others paralyzed by polio.

To me and to so many who had polio, Roosevelt is a heroic figure. Happening upon his nautical log was especially thrilling. I too love fishing, I too love the water.

What follows is FDR's *Larooco* log. The entries concentrate on the usual subjects of nautical logs——weather, route, fish caught, broken engines, guests, meals. I've interspersed them with notes and illustrations concerning people aboard the boat or events in the world outside the *Larooco,* a world in which FDR would play such a decisive role not too many years later. Scattered throughout are uncaptioned snapshots taken during the *Larooco* cruises. In the original log, these photographs are pasted onto ten pages with almost no identification of people, places, or dates. A complete facsimile of the log follows the afterword.

For the most part, Roosevelt used initials in the entries to indicate someone's identity, but for the sake of clarity, I've substituted the full names wherever possible. In some entries, in order to make the log more approachable, I have condensed or omitted sentences, changed their order, and laid Roosevelt's words out in the form of poems, but the words are all his own. My purpose was to make the text sonorous as well as draw the reader in. These edited entries contain almost no punctuation. All the entries that contain full punctuation are FDR's words untouched. May the shifting forms increase the log's glow. Welcome aboard, Reader.

THE *LAROOCO* LOG

1924

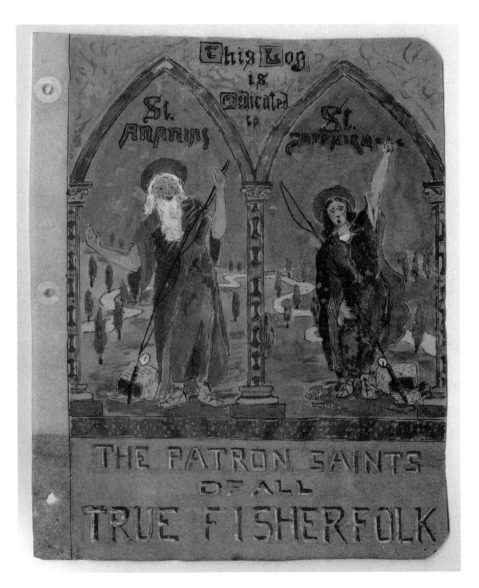

Louis Howe's colorful painting for the log, with its dedication to Ananias and Sapphira, the patron saints of lying fishermen.

R U L E S
For log-book scribes

I.

This Log Book must be entirely accurate and truthful. In putting down weights and numbers of fish, however, the following tables may be used.

Weights.
2 oz. make—1 log book pound
5 log book pounds make—"a large fish"
2 "large fish" make—"A record day's catch"

Measures.
2 inches make—1 log book foot
2 log book feet make—"Big as a whale"
Anything above "whale" size may be described
as an "Icthyosaurus"

(Note—In describing fish that got away, all these measures may be doubled—it is also permitted, when over 30 seconds are required to pull in a fish to say "After half an hour's hard fighting—."

II.

The poetically inclined are warned that LAROOCO does not rhyme with Morocco. Also the combinations "knows I felt" to rhyme with Roosevelt and "Saw hence" to rhyme with Lawrence are not permitted.

III.

Verbatim reports of the private conversations of the chief engineer with his carburetor must be represented only thus – "x ! ! x ! — ? ? X ! —."

IV.

All references to "community life" must be written in code.

V.

The leaves of this Log are made to be easily removed. All frank opinions as to the character, habits and general personality of one's shipmates written after a 3 days' nor'wester and no fish will be so removed.

Saturday, February 2

At Jacksonville, Florida, FDR went on board and put Larooco in commission. Sailing-master Robert S. Morris and Mrs. Morris spent the day getting provisions, and the trunks, etc. were duly unpacked, fishing gear stowed and Library of World's Worst Literature placed on shelves.

Sunday, February 3

Gave all hands opportunity to go to Church. No takers. Hence left dock at 11:30 a.m. proceeding down to St. John's River, about 18 miles, thence South into Canal. Very narrow channel and little water. Most of the way a straight cut through pine lands. Moored to old piling at 5:30 p.m., 2 or 3 miles short of the Toll Chain. Pondered deeply over interior decorations (of boat—not self)—green or light blue—or both?

Lenin dies on January 21, and Stalin begins to take over Russia. Nine days later, FDR turns forty-two years old, and three days after that, he begins the Larooco log.

Monday, February 4

Marshy river
Strong headwind

Anchored at St. Augustine

Hard rain late afternoon
Delicious oysters and whitefish
New leaks in cabin and my stateroom

Tuesday, February 5

Yesterday when approaching town
we saw flags
at half mast—President Wilson
died Sunday morning

Wednesday, February 6

Underway at St. Augustine
south through drawbridge

Steering cable slipped
Blew sideways onto sand bar

Tide going out
Larooco soon high and dry

Maunsell, Missy and FDR
went fishing—one sea trout

Large flock of black skimmers
Flock of Greater Snow Goose

All hands played solitaire
Incoming tide lifted Larooco clear

Maunsell Crosby, a good friend and neighbor from Rhinebeck, New York. A serious ornithologist, he went on collecting expeditions for the Museum of Natural History. Before he joined FDR on the boat, Roosevelt wrote to him, "As to clothing—I can assure you it is of the simplest. I live in old flannel trousers and a flannel or tennis shirt, depending on the degree of warmth. Nothing like a dinner coat or even white flannel trousers is countenanced."[1]

Thursday, February 7

Stopped by ship in Canal
Freight boat aground

Seven other boats
lined up

Wind had driven
the water out

Franklin D. Roosevelt, former assistant secretary of the navy and who was democratic candidate for the vice presidency in 1920, is just folks, too, and when he plays he plays the way just folks would play. He caught by the photographer yesterday in an unguarded moment aboard his yacht Larooca, where he had spread tarpaulin on the deck and was busy plying brush, re-furbishing some of the furniture. Mr. Roosevelt has just returned from a fishing cruise in the Florida Keys. He is making his headquarters in Miami. Photograph by The Miami Herald.

The Miami Herald *takes note of Roosevelt's presence, calling him "just folks," playing the way "just folks play, refurbishing furniture aboard his yacht."*

Missy and FDR
in launch fishing

No luck

Painted ¾ of a chair—
booful blue

Friday, February 8

Wind still N.W.
No chance of release today
The "Lounger III" belonging to
some Uppercu persons
tried to be smart
and rude
by pushing by us
Stuck in sand
Bent propeller
Just desserts etc.

Saturday, February 9

Very cold night. Waited for N.E. wind to blow some more water into the
ridiculous Canal. At 4 p.m. the freight boat got through, then the Lounger, then
"Larooco" and the second boat back of us stuck. We were lucky to get ahead, but
in a few minutes the port shaft hit a rock and bent. Tied up at the toll bridge
5 miles South.

Sunday, February 10

A little warmer
Passed into Halifax River

Reached Ormonde Bridge
Draw out of order!

At 4:30 at last
Through the draw

Anchored off Daytona
at dark

Maunsell ashore
Brought sad news of death of Missy's father

Monday, February 11

Party broken up by Missy's departure
Clutch of port engine on the blink
One thing after another

Missy LeHand, left. "Cleopatra" is written on the right-hand photo, and beneath it, "friend of M.A.L." (Missy's initials). Who is this Cleopatra, costumed as the alluring ancient woman who used her charms to influence powerful men?

Tuesday, February 12

Uneventful day
Engines recovered from pneumonia
Left Daytona

Kept on South
till we stuck in the mud
before the "Haul-Over"

Anchored for night
Much playing
solitaire and Parcheesi

George Gershwin's Rhapsody in Blue *premieres at Carnegie Hall as FDR and friends pass the evening playing Parcheesi. Perhaps they sang* Home on the Range *that night, at one time FDR's favorite song.*

Wednesday, February 13

Stopped at Haul-Over
for very superior eggs

Came into broad expanse
of Indian River
Kept on

A fine day's run

Thursday, February 14

Yesterday Maunsell took a bath
Reason clothed in mystery
Now it develops that today
is his Birthday

Having no other gifts
I took a bath also
in his honor
It is a heavenly warm day
shirtsleeve weather

We painted two dining room chairs blue
Proceeded ever Southward
Anchored off Fort Pierce at 6 p.m.
Had cake and some flowers
for the Birthday dinner

This Indian River
is a wonderful body of water
stretching N. and S. for miles and
separated by a narrow stretch of
beach from the ocean
Shallow almost everywhere

Friday, February 15

It is a wonderful hot day—we are getting to the nearest point to the Gulf Stream. At 3, while passing through Peck Lake we ran aground and stuck aft. Engines would not move her. Channel 50 feet wide. We got our hawser to a mangrove tree and by the united efforts of the engines and Mac in the motor boat and the Capt. and Maunsell and Roan on the windlass she came off in an hour. Passed through the lovely winding Lower Jupiter Narrows into Hobe Sound where we anchored for the night off the Olympia Beach Club.

Saturday, February 16

Left Olympia of the Very Mortals
at 9:30 and took our time
going aground two or three times

Reaching
Palm Beach
at 4

Maunsell ashore
for papers
and mail

Spent hours trying to find out
why the world continues to move on
in our absence

Sunday, February 17

In the morning Maunsell and I went ashore and motored all over Palm Beach for an hour; not having been here since 1904 I found the growth of mushroom millionaires' houses luxuriant. The women we saw went well with the place—

The Lost Generation, a group of American literary expatriates, flourishes in Paris as Roosevelt cruises the Florida waters. Here Gertrude Stein plays with Ernest Hemingway's son in a Parisian park. Stein wrote, "Everybody is contemporary with his period. . . . The thing that is important is that nobody knows what the contemporariness is. In other words, they don't know where they are going, but they are on their way."[2]

and we desired to meet them no more than we wished to remain in the harbor even an hour more than necessary. Up anchor at 1 and with starboard engine running well and port engine coughing spasmodically we got down to the South end of Lake Worth and anchored for the night.

Monday, February 18

During the night
we dragged

All hands called
to get her underway
into the channel

Boulders along it
and in it

Tied up in Canal
above
Hillsboro Inlet

Tuesday, February 19

Maunsell to date has seen 98 different varieties of birds. He had a walk ashore last evening and added 8 species. We ran aground six times today—very bad water—at one place, just below New River Inlet, the yacht Capts. accuse the local Fort Lauderdale people with dumping rocks into the channel to make repairs necessary and bring trade! Painted chairs most of the p.m. We had to wait just below the inlet for 3 hours till the tide rose.

Wednesday, February 20

Dumbfoundling Lake—well named
Ran aground

Port engine
in comatose condition

Blew into bushes
Broke two windows

Barge towed us four miles
Anchored
Bad rain squalls

Started at 4
Moored to dock up Miami River

Miami or Bust
Bust lost

Thursday, February 21

Miami. Maunsell shopped, opened bank account for me etc. in the morning. Engine doctor began diagnosis. In p.m. with Maunsell motored to Miami Beach, called on the James M. Cox's who were out, went to Cocoanut Grove, called on Wm. J. Bryan, who came out to the car and we had a nice talk.

FDR was Cox's vice-presidential running mate in 1920; they lost the election to Warren G. Harding. Earlier, FDR had served as assistant secretary of the navy in Woodrow Wilson's cabinet, along with Secretary of State William Jennings Bryan of "Cross of Gold" fame. Though his focus was on his legs, FDR rarely passed up a chance for political hobnobbing during the Larooco years.

Friday, February 22

Miami Engine doctor at work

Patient may respond to
heroic treatment

In launch ran down to Bear Cut
Trolled for an hour

Got one mackerel
Ashore for lunch

Maunsell and I took off all raiment
and swam—for two hours lay on the sand

Friday, February 22
Excerpted from a letter:

Dearest Mama,

. . . Today Maunsell and I took the motor boat to an inlet, fished, got out on the sandy beach, picnicked and swam and lay in the sun for hours. I know it is doing the legs good, and though I have worn the braces hardly at all, I get lots of exercise crawling around, and I know the muscles are better than ever before.[3]

Saturday, February 23

Hard work making boat spic and span
Grand tea party in p.m.

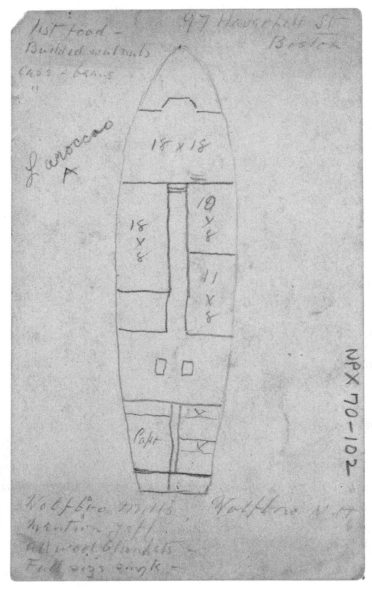

When Missy first arrived on the boat, FDR showed her his large stateroom and a small one opposite his, for her. The two shared a bathroom. Earlier, Roosevelt described the boat's layout in a letter to John Lawrence. "Beginning at the stern she has the usual little 'back porch' like the WEONA, then crew quarters for 4, then a very large engine room with gallies on one side. Forward of this is a passageway—on the port side a bathroom and large stateroom with a double brass bed in it. On the starboard side 2 staterooms with 2 bunks each. At the forward end of the passageway is a short flight of steps going up into the living room, which occupies the whole forward, end and has 2 big windows on each side and 3 windows forward where the wheel is. From the living room another short flight of steps goes up to the top deck, which is equipped with awnings."[4]

Gov and Mrs. Cox, Tim Ansberry
Ed. N. Hurley, Col. and
Mrs. Van Tassel

Missy poured tea
Maunsell mixed Larooco drinks

Missy was back aboard the Larooco *after an absence of almost two weeks. Eleanor wrote to FDR, "I haven't told Mama [FDR's mother] that Missy is back because I think she has more peace of mind when she doesn't know things!" Sara was not pleased that Missy was the hostess on the boat and that Eleanor, on the rare occasions when she visited, was a guest.*[5]

Sunday, February 24

We all went down
to Bear Cut
in the launch

Fished in rain
Landed at Beach
Had lunch

Grand swimming party
followed by sun bath
Home at 5

Final Parcheesi match
and Maunsell left
Will miss him much

Monday, February 25

Missy and Mrs. Morris ashore shopping. In the p.m. a drive to Miami Beach to call on J.C. Penney etc.

Tuesday, February 26

Tied up at dock
all day
Engine repairs

Too much wind
to go down
Biscayne Bay anyway

Wednesday, February 27

Went down the Bay
Anchored inside Pumpkin Key
close to mouth of Angelfish Creek

Pangs of Mal de Mer for Missy
Blew hard
Gave us a good roll

Thursday, February 28

Went in launch with Mac and Missy to get mail etc. at Key Largo. On way down were greatly delayed by trolling and failing to find entrance to Jewfish Creek. Finally started on return trip at 6:30 p.m. It was dark by the time we got out of Jewfish Creek. Steered by the stars for the South entrance of Steamboat Creek—missed it—passing it at least three times within 100 feet in the dark. Gave it up at 9 P.M. Tried to find the channels W. of the Island, found one line of stakes—lost the next—aground badly three or four times, got through at last—made Pumpkin Key by great luck and ran into Angelfish Creek without even seeing the marker which we must have passed within 50 feet. Back on board at 11:30 p.m.!

Friday, February 29

Recuperating at Angelfish after yesterday's adventures. Caught a few small fish.

Saturday, March 1

Went back to Key Largo in the launch, taking lunch with us this time, caught no fish, but found a lot of mail. Got back in time for one of Mrs. Morris's delightful suppers.

Sunday, March 2

A lovely warm lazy day. Fished for angelfish, grunts, etc. and got enough for a meal.

Monday, March 3

Left Angelfish Creek after breakfast
Ran through to Miami in 5½ hours
Tied up in the River

Tuesday, March 4

Sad news
John Lawrence
1/2 owner and partner in this ancient craft
cannot join us

Before this first cruise FDR had written Lawrence urging him to come south.

Hyde Park
December 5, 1923

Dear John:
That brief sketch of your situation carrying you to South America, Paris, Pacific Coast, Greece and all way stations makes me think that you need to change your doctor and again come under the tender ministrations of old Dr. Roosevelt. He will, therefore, give you the following perfectly firm and equally well-meant advice!

I.
You are no longer young, as you and I have learned from our children.

II.
You have never given yourself a real chance since that last operation!

III.

You will not go through bankruptcy if you take a real holiday.

IV.

The business will survive during your absence. It is one of the horrible comments on the indispensableness of each of us that the foregoing is true in every indispensable businessman's business that we know of.

V.

"The only way to resume is to resume"—i.e., if you will cut yourself off from home, business, and all worries completely for 2 months I will guarantee to <u>bore</u> you back to good health on the LAROOCO. For the first two weeks you will try to go out fishing every morning before sunrise. The rest of the day you will be planning new adventures. For the next two weeks you will be sitting around wondering whether the cotton business still survives. It will take you this first month to get it out of your system. The 2nd month you won't care whether the fish bite or not, you will have forgotten the business of cotton, ladies' underwear, etc. and will be sitting around on that top deck drinking in nature (and probably other things too) with complete satisfaction to your mind and body.

Honestly, all joking aside, the LAROOCO is just what you need . . .

As ever yours,
Franklin D. Roosevelt[6]

A month later, he again pressed Lawrence to visit.

Happy New Year to you and yours. Do, if you can, come down before Mar 1st. If you like, you can tell your business associates that I am dying and have sent for you to come in a hurry and hold my hand in my last moments.[7]

Wednesday, March 5

Wire from Eleanor

Anna
cannot come
but
Elliott will
Another tea party
on deck

Discussion of
cows
boy-scouts
and politics

Thursday, March 6

Ran down the bay
to Barnes Sound
Anchored between
Steamboat
and Jewfish

Caught
a nice mess
of crawfish

Friday, March 7

Moved into
Jewfish Creek

Rain
high wind
engine trouble

Saturday, March 8

Left Jewfish Creek about 11, lunched on deck enroute, and got down to the mouth of Tavernier Creek about 4. The Captain went ashore, got mail and some provisions.

Sunday, March 9

As a blow threatened we moved Larooco into Tavernier Creek. Eleanor Hennessey, Missy, and FDR went through the creek to the Ocean and landed at the Albury's little dock at Tavernier. Almost all inhabitants of the settlement are Alburys—those not so named are at least close relatives. We swam in the p.m.

Monday, March 10

Blew too hard
to go fishing
on reef
So we
fished
the creek

Swam again
at delightful
beach

Tuesday, March 11

All hands
went reef fishing
in Albury's launch

Pretty rough

Wednesday, March 12

Miss Hennessy left us at noon—very sad not to be able to wait to meet the attractions of Davis who comes next Sunday.

Thursday, March 13

Blowing hard all day. Stayed in creek.

Livingston Davis, an old college friend, with FDR ten years earlier.

Friday, March 14

Ditto. This year has been a very poor one as to weather down here—a lot of wind, large temperature changes etc.

Saturday, March 15

A grand fishing party
to the reef
in the launch

20 Barracuda
Cero Mackerel and
Spanish Mackerel

Mrs. Morris caught several

Sunday, March 16

Livingston Davis arrived at 1
weighted down
with sundry wet and dry goods

Looks like a sick child
He's recuperating from shingles
bunions boils and cold in the head

A blowy day
Stayed in Tavernier Creek
Livingston unpacking fishing gear
I making boats

FDR loved building model boats, which he would sometimes enter in races on the Hudson River. Here he is in 1920 on a boat in the Bay of Fundy with his sons James and Elliott and their model boats.

Monday, March 17

Water too cold to swim
Wind too high to go to reef

Livingston went to R.R. bridge
to fish
To the disgust of the ladies
Came back minus trousers

He had exercised earlier
on the top deck a la nature

Why do people who *must* take off their clothes
go anywhere where the other sex is present

Capt. remarked some men get shot for less

Tuesday, March 18

To the reef with Livingston in M.L. Albury's launch. At Pickles reef we found a lee from the swell and got all the fishing we wanted. Caught in all—35 fish—L.D. 17 and F.D.R. 18—mostly Cero Mackerel and Barracuda—but including 2 Yellow

Mackerel

Jacks and several Spanish Mackerel. A shark took a mackerel I was bringing in and I played him for several minutes before he went off with my fish, spoon, and wire inside of him. Our day's catch ran well over 250 pounds of fish.

Wednesday, March 19

Livingston went off
alone with Albury
to the stream

Gone all day

Very hot and
the mosquitos began

So at noon
we moved Larooco
out of the Creek

Thursday, March 20

After lunch fished with Albury for small grunts
and sailor's-choice off Tavernier Key on the Ocean side

On return we picked up Mrs. Albury and Marjorie aged 4
to show them the Larooco

When we got to her a heavy storm approached from the West
We tried to get up anchor but
in backing the rowboat swamped

Her insides scattered broadcast over the waters
Albury picked them up

Then his painter got foul of our port propeller
Hell to pay

Davis got the awning off but had to disrobe to do it
as it was raining

We got out the other anchor
Tied everything down
Trusted to Heaven that she wouldn't blow ashore

Mrs. Albury and the little girl stayed on board
Slept on the cot and mattress on the living room floor

Friday, March 21

Mac ashore in the launch to get mail
Held up by tide at RR bridge
All day it blew a gale

6:30 he showed up
Stopped his engine too soon
then couldn't start it
Drifted off into the darkness

Capt. Morris rowed downwind
Found him aground

All this day
we feared she would drift
or the anchor chain go
but she has come through
and the wind is dying down

Saturday, March 22

Wind much moderated. Engines both working. Off early.

There are no entries in the log from March 23 to April 4, with no explanation. It is unlikely that FDR was distracted by events in Russia, where Stalin had slowly been consolidating his power in the months since Lenin's death. It is equally unlikely that he knew that Adolf Hitler had been sentenced to five years on April 1 for his participation in the Beer Hall Putsch of November 1923, much less that Hitler would begin writing Mein Kampf (My Struggle) *during his imprisonment. Even more unlikely is that FDR took note of the birth of Marlon Brando on April 3, to an unconventional Jazz Age mother who drove cars, wore trousers, and smoked and drank heavily.*

Saturday, April 5

Livingston Davis waved from the train for Key West
Seen by Mrs. Morris who shook a towel in reply

After lunch Missy, Mrs. Morris and I
went to Ocean side of Long Key

Had a fine bathe in shallow water
Sharks playing outshore from us

Sunday, April 6

A quiet morning answering mail
Exercising with canes and crutches

In the p.m. Missy and I
went up and down the Trestle
in the launch with the Captain

At the start
I hooked a tarpon
on a spoon
on my light rod and reel
with no brakes

He jumped twice
took out 200 feet of line
burned a bad blister
on my thumb
but was still on

I got him in a little
He jumped again
Ran out

I stopped him
by letting the handle
of the reel
bump past my palm

He was on for 8 minutes
then the hook pulled out!

Looked like a fish
of 30 pounds

That was only the start

In a few minutes
I landed a Kingfish
Missy got a grouper
next a very big snapper
then we ended up with two jacks
another grouper
another snapper
and two Spanish Mackerel

 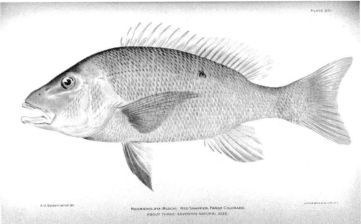

Snowy Grouper and Red Snapper

At 8 p.m. after dark
the Albury launch
turned up
in a rough sea
with Albury's brother

Capt. Morris
"heard a squawk"
asked what that was
Albury answered
"I've got my wife and baby"

So here is the whole family
wife 17 years old
baby 16 months

They are about to go to bed in the guest stateroom

Monday, April 7

Missy went to pay bill
at the Fishing Camp

At 2:30 got underway
starboard engine
running fitfully

The launch lashed
to port side
the little motor
pushing astern

We ambled along
near McGinty Key
and anchored for the night

Tuesday, April 8

A heavenly day. Under way at 8, and anchored off Tavernier-landside at 10—We had a grand swim while the Capt. and young Albury went ashore. Mr. M. Albury, the storekeeper, came over to the beach and we had a long talk about the possibility of his starting a gas, water and yacht supply base at Tavernier. At 1:30 M.R. Albury came on board with his wife and Marjorie, 4 years old, grand chance to go free to Miami! They were given the guest stateroom! We started and kept on going without a hitch, through Jewfish drawbridge and anchored for the night in Barnes Sound.

Wednesday, April 9

At 7:30 Missy and Mrs. Morris went to Key Largo to see if any telegrams were there and to tip the telegraph man, Mr. Barcus, who has been very kind. We got underway at 10 and had a splendid run with the wind aft. Starboard engine running well and the Albury launch pushing on the port side. Just before we got to the channel two miles S. of Miami the launch engine went wrong and we anchored for the night.

Thursday, April 10

Started on the last leg of the cruise
Just after we rounded the point to go
into the Miami River
the steering cable broke
but we had enough headway
to get to the Royal Palm dock

The good old craft is thus safely moored
after many adventures
The engines have of course

given all sorts of trouble
In fact they have been the source
of every untoward happening
but we knew when she started from N.Y.
that the engines were old and would give trouble
and only people with bad indigestion
chronic grouch or bad nerves worried
when things went a little less smoothly
than if we had the engines running right

"She is the most comfortable boat imaginable," FDR wrote to John Lawrence the following autumn, "I enjoyed every moment of my two months on her.

"The engines were, of course, a hopeless failure, but we knew that this would be so when we bought her. The run south just about finished them, and the result was that the rest of the time I had to limp along as best I could, but as I was in no hurry I was amused rather than put out by the various balks—first of one engine and then the other—and did not mind it in the least."[8]

Friday, April 11

Seeing people
laying up Larooco
putting new engines
in her

Started packing
putting away linen
china, etc.

In the p.m.
went in the launch
to Bear's Cut
Had a fine swim

Saturday, April 12

To Bear's Cut again in the launch for a swim. Busy packing
and getting ready to go out of commission.

Sunday, April 13

Capt. and Mrs. Morris
Missy and I
went to Bear's Cut
for a picnic lunch and final swim

At sundown
Larooco went out of commission

Larooco goes to yard tomorrow
Will be cared for
during summer
by Atlantic Boat Works

So ends Cruise No. 1

1925

After FDR put the Larooco *in drydock in the spring of 1924, he leaves "My-am-eye," as he jokingly calls Miami, and returns to his life in the north, where Eleanor is becoming more active in the political arena. There is much to take note of over the months before his return to the boat.*

On May 10, 1924, J. Edgar Hoover is appointed director of the FBI, a position he will hold until his death in 1972. He despised Eleanor's liberal bent and in later years directed the FBI to keep a close eye on her.

FDR cannot resist entering the national public arena for the first time since his illness. On June 26, at the Democratic Convention, he gives a speech nominating Al Smith, governor of New York, for the party's presidential candidate. The party is badly split, and Governor Smith does not receive the nomination. The moment, however, is pivotal for Roosevelt as he uses his crutches to make his way across the stage. The crowd goes wild as he reaches the podium.

On August 5, FDR picnics with Eleanor and her close friends Marion Dickerman and Nancy Cook in Hyde Park, New York, near Springwood, the house he was born in. He offers to design and build them a "honeymoon cottage" nearby.

On October 4, FDR takes his first swim at Warm Springs, Georgia. The Atlanta Journal covers his visit by running a special in their Sunday magazine of October 26 that is syndicated all over the country, prompting many requests from polio patients to visit Warm Springs. This photo was taken later.

On January 14, 1925, Bessie Smith and Louis Armstrong record "St. Louis Blues" as the Jazz Age flourishes. Years later, after the Great Depression hits, Smith records "Nobody Knows You When You're Down and Out" and Armstrong sings "The W.P.A." to celebrate President Roosevelt's Works Project Administration, which put millions of unemployed people back to work.

On January 24, 1925, Al Capone, the gangster known as Scarface, takes over the Chicago crime family. On December 8, 1941, after the Japanese attack on Pearl Harbor, President Roosevelt will ride in Capone's armored Cadillac Town Sedan to deliver his Day of Infamy speech to Congress. The car, impounded by the Treasury Department after Capone's 1931 arrest, was brought out to protect the president from any potential assassination attempt.

1925
Larooco
Cruise Number Two

Foreword

During the past summer and autumn Larooco was laid up at Atlantic Boat Yard, Miami, and was re-engined with 2 Regal Motors. Also the steering wheel was shifted from fore cabin to top deck, and new electric light motor was installed.

The new work seems to be right, but the Yard took very bad care of the boat. Chairs and various small articles were stolen. New canvas was laid over whole top deck. Capt. and Mrs. Morris went on board to live the end of November and helped get things in shape for going into commission.

Wednesday, February 4

FDR arrived Miami
Train 24 hours late
due to floods in Georgia
and vagaries of R.R.

Went straight
on board
and Larooco
went into commission

Thursday, February 5

More shopping, replacing stolen furniture (at expense of yard) and laying in supplies. In the afternoon the Executive Council of the Am. Fed. of Labor with wives etc., thirty in all, came on board and I had interesting talk with William Green, the President, and other leaders.

FDR has only been on the boat for a day when he is mingling with labor leaders. His dedication to and mutual romance with the labor movement blossoms later. This poster, from the Jewish Daily Forward of November 1, 1936, shows him with a stalwart worker.

Friday, February 6

More shopping etc. Bought a new rowboat to replace the one stolen.

Saturday, February 7

After filling up with water and gas, got underway at 12:30 and proceeded down Biscayne Bay. Engines working finely. Ran into Angelfish Creek and tied up to bushes at 5:15 p.m. LeRoy Jones caught the first fish, a mangrove snapper, and enough others were caught by him and Monty Snyder to give us a meal tomorrow.

Sunday, February 8

Quiet day in Angelfish Creek
After lunch Missy and I
out in launch

Caught a big Angelfish
3 snappers
a large turbot
and 2 grunts

Monday, February 9

Had a quick run through Jewfish Creek
getting to Tavernier at 1:15
FDR steered most of the way

Had a good swim in the afternoon
Sent ashore for mail

The Aquarium on top deck—
two wooden tubs—
did not work
Fish dead in the morning
Too many of them in it

Tuesday, February 10

Sent off
a lot of mail
Had a morning swim

Took launch
through creek
to Albury's
on the Ocean side
Saw most of the tribe

Arranged for them
to take the black kitten
daughter of Tweetie
last year's houseboat guest

Too rough
for outside fishing
so we came back

Wednesday, February 11

A violent thunderstorm and very heavy rain at 5 a.m. Too cold to swim today. At 1 went through Creek and out to Couch Reef with young Lou, an Albury nephew. Got some fine Barracuda fishing, over a dozen and all large size. F.D.R. landed a 35 pounder with 12 thread line and a light rod and reel without any brake on it. On way back a heavy squall with rain broke on us, we transferred to our launch at the Albury dock and came through the Creek, darkness and rain not withstanding. Found Larooco near W. mouth of Creek, pounding heavily. Came along side, Missy climbed on board safely, F.D.R. fell on floor of pounding launch and tore knee ligaments. Had to be passed in through galley window. Heavy wind and rain all night, but anchors held.

Thursday, February 12

FDR's leg possibly broken so got underway at 10 and ran till dark getting within 2 hours of Miami.

Friday, February 13

Reached Miami at 11 a.m.
Missy ashore for Doctor
who came on board

Diagnosed torn
and pulled ligaments
Strapped leg up

Tried in vain
to locate Maunsell
but he had left
for Tavernier
to find us

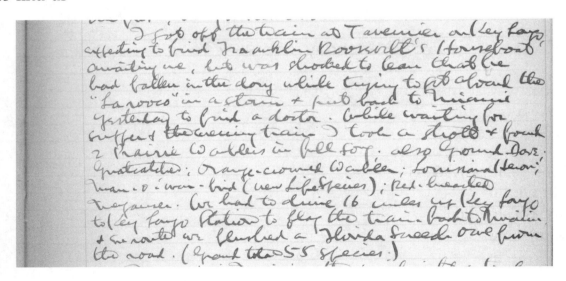

Maunsell Crosby's bird log entry for February 13, 1925.

Saturday, February 14

At 1 a.m. a shout
from Royal Palm Dock
announced arrival
of Maunsell Crosby
who had gone to Tavernier
found our message and come back

Slept late

Had visits from Mort Newhall
Col. Van Tassel and M. Helm
the two latter in real estate

Sunday, February 15

A quiet day. Got off mail. Doctor Turner came and reported
FDR's knee mending slowly. F.D.R. still in bed.

Monday, February 16

Under way at 10:30
made a fine run
to Tarpan Basin

Capt. Charles Watkins
will pilot us
Act as fish guide
below Long Key

After dark
they got us
a fine mess
of crawfish
and a Grouper
for chowder

Parcheesi Contest
actively under way

Tuesday, February 17

Reached Tavernier at 11

Maunsell and the Capt.
got mail
some eggs and
2 live chickens

FDR got stiff brace on leg
and was carried on deck

Arrived Long Key at 4

Wednesday, February 18

Went to dock for gas
Ran down to anchorage inside of Channel Key
as it looks like a Norther

```
                                        xxxxxxxxxxx
                                        55 Liberty St.

                                                  at Long Key, Florida,
                                                  February 19, 1925.

          Miami Grocery Company,
          Miami, Florida.

          Gentlemen:

                    Will you kindly send to me at Long Key, Florida on

          the morning train Monday, February 23d, the following:

          12 grape fruit              1200 lbs ice
          24 oranges                  4 boxes saltines
          1 cocktail sauce            3 lbs coffee
          4 doz. eggs                 2 guava jellies
          2 Fly-tox                   2 cream cheeses
          1 corn flakes
          6 cans milk                 5 lbs sausage (not most expensive
          3 lbs butter                                 ones)
          10 lbs. sugar               8 lbs very good rump corn beef
          3 anghovie paste            2 broilers
          12 loaves bread             12 pork chops
          2 boxes yellow corn meal    12 lamb chops
                                      small ham


                    From the last box of fruit which we got we threw away

          15 oranges and 6 grape fruit, so will you please send us fruit

          which is not too ripe, and which is good and solid.    Also,

          will you try to get for us a really good piece of corned beef.

                                             Very truly yours,
```

FDR's grocery list.

Thursday, February 19

Tom Lynch arrived safely on board about 9:30 a.m. looking pale (see below). Got under way and ran down to Knights Key, anchoring N. of track inside Hog Key. After lunch Maunsell and Tom went fishing and brought back a large mess of fish—2 jacks, 1 grouper—2 porgies and over 20 grunts.

Friday, February 20

At anchor Hog Key. Missy and Tom went fishing—1 jack—and Tom looks less pale. An enormous mess of crawfish in eve.

Saturday, February 21

Back to Long Key after lunch. Got mail and ran down to Channel Key. Tom no longer pale, is in fact putting anything on his face which his friends suggest.

As the Larooco *plies Channel Key, Harold Ross launches the* New Yorker *magazine. Eight years later, FDR almost makes the cover for March 4, 1933, driving to his inauguration with Herbert Hoover, his predecessor. A failed assassination attempt on FDR's life nixes the cover.*

Sunday, February 22, Birthington's Washday

Frances de Rham
arrived 3 hours late
Was met by gents
in launch

She caught her lunch
on way back
She also looks pale
Tom at opposite extreme

After lunch
all off to Duck Key

Swam in shallow water
among the sponges

Business of washing
each other's backs
with sea soap

After grog Missy and Frances
rowed over to "Whileaway"
and nearly got more

Monday, February 23

Another washday
All much disturbed at night by Maunsell
who dreamed he was a Pink Bazoo

J. S. L.
F. D. R.

To
M. S. Crosby
Companionable Ornithologist. "LAROOCO"

Oh the Blue Laroo is missing you
For you taught her things no boat e'er knew
Of the martin purple and heron blue,
And the ways and wiles of the things thatflew

So she slipped her cable one day and went
Down Biscayne Bay on a hunt intent,
Her engines were wheezy, her crank shaft bent
And what the captain was saying he meant!

She bumped a marker and grazed a shoal,
And tried to occupy nearly the whole
Of the big wide Bay. She tried to roll -
And the skipper yelled "I've lost control!"

Oh the Blue Laroo went down the Bay
Like a streak of light at the break of day.
The other boats gave her "right of way
And manned the rail and yelled "hurray".

The engines just wouldn't reverse at all -
And the speed grew greater in spite of the
                              call
Of the owner and captain - they wouldn't stall -
And the crew began to howl and bawl.

Her speed got up to 20 knots
Then 30, and 40 - and that's a lot.
The scenery passed like blurs and blots.
Her progress was marked by dashes and dots.

They gave up every effort to steer
And clung to the rail as they saw her clear
The water. But they raised a cheer
As she rose in the air without check or fear.

Then off on the farthest horizon rim
They saw a shpe in the ether dim -
A huge bird soaring with plumage trim
Dipping to meet each zephyr's whim.

The Blue Laroo rose up to see
This new companion, and to be
It's fellow in the heavens free -
A new bird species ! - Hully gee!

You ask what was this species new,
And rare, and bright and gorgeous too?
Why, what would charm the Blue Laroo
Except the lovely Pink Bazoo?

(FDR)

FDR's poem for Maunsell Crosby.

FDR and Frances de Rham. A childhood friend known for her beauty, she was married to Henry de Rham, a college friend of FDR's.

Ran up to Long Key and took on water and gas
before which Frances and Maunsell and Tom thoroughly
explored Channel Key which we have determined to own

They planted three coconuts near landing
and brought back corcooloulus minor and other flora
Parcheesi tournament is progressing in favor of Missy

Tom has kindly consented the use of his face
in place of the port running light
It will save oil

In p.m. took launch around to E. of Long Key and all swam
Tom caught 1 jack and 1 grouper on return trip
and FDR nearly got one about 6 inches long

Grog in midst of glorious sunset
which was almost as poetic in coloring
as Frances' and Missy's nighties

Colors remained hoisted
Much complaint—Answer "We're loadin' ice."
Roy rescued our nautical reputation

From February 24 to March 23, the log is kept by others aboard the boat, as is clear from the different handwritings, though it isn't clear who wrote what or why FDR stopped keeping the log himself. The entries include the boat's route, weather, fish caught, food, drink, games, visitors, engine trouble, as well as daily goings-on—sewing, working on a stamp collection, knitting, storytelling, discussing books, even sharing dreams. Below are a few excerpts.

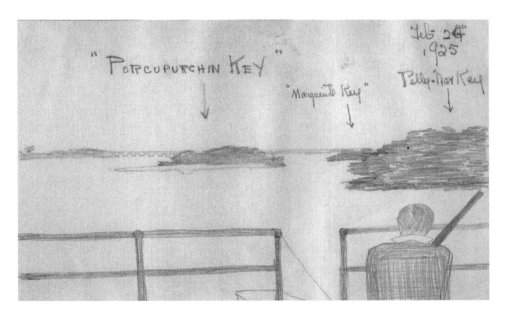

This drawing, dated February 24, 1925, is glued onto the log's pages of photographs.

March 1

Everyone has now read "Gone Native."

This work of fiction by Robert James Fletcher, with the subtitle A Tale of the South Seas, *had come out the year before.*

March 6

Reading aloud choice bits from Mark Twain's Auto.

March 17

The rest lounge about the deck and spend most of their time discussing what the first chapter of the "Green Hat" is really about!

This sentimental best-selling novel by Michael Arlen, full of rebellion and cynicism, takes place in Europe.

Reflecting a complex and questionable blitheness on the subject of Jews, one entry writer says, "(we'd) do some real fishing of 'Jew' (meaning Jewfish)." Another entry describes a new visitor to the Larooco *as "a pale faced descendant of Adam who after having some of the spirit of the ship [poured or injected into him] was identified as Julian Goldman."*

Goldman, a close friend of FDR's, owned a chain of department stores. Roosevelt was his lawyer. During World War II, when FDR did not bomb the railroad tracks leading to Auschwitz, Goldman stopped speaking to him.

In early March, Eleanor made a rare visit to the boat and stayed for an unprecedented ten days to celebrate a special occasion. Louis Howe, intimate friend and advisor to both Eleanor and Franklin, was on the boat then too, often painting watercolors for the log, including one of a hooked-nose jewfish.

Tuesday March 17

Much festivity in the evening due to the fact that it is the 20th wedding anniversary of the FDRs. Special green paper table cloth, place cards, and refreshments! Moving speech by Henry Morgenthau Jr. and presentation to the Hon. FDR of 2 pair of linen panties.

The joking couple, soon after they married—Eleanor drinks a cocktail while Franklin knits.

Eleanor left the Larooco *the day after the anniversary party, and FDR resumed writing in the log a week later, as his son James came on board.*

Tuesday, March 24

Left Channel Key at noon, soon after arrival of James, who came from Groton. After lunch fished the trestle and Henry Morgenthau got a 12 pound Jack and James a Mackerel. In the p.m. the clouds came up and fearing a Norther we ran up to Jewfish Creek anchorage. The H. Morgenthau Jr.'s left at 7 p.m. in the dory and got soaked on their way to Long Key in the dory to take the train. Heavy rain but not much wind.

FDR with his old friend and neighbor Henry Morgenthau Jr. Morgenthau, grandson of German Jewish immigrants and son of an ambassador, was FDR's secretary of the treasury during the New Deal. After World War II, he was instrumental in helping Jewish refugees and limiting Germany's future military power.

Wednesday, March 25

At Jewfish Key
James and I
fished the trestle
got a mess of bottom fish

At 6, Fortuna with R. Talbot
Judge Corrigan
Judge Fred Kernochan
Dr. Rushmore
Willy Post and Gallatin Pell
anchored near us

A fine poker party

Thursday, March 26

Ran back to Long Key
to get last mail

Headed North
on homeward journey

Getting to Tavernier Creek
at four

Friday, March 27

Jimmy and I left with
Rodney Albury in latter's launch

Ran to Couch Reef
and started fishing

Sea too much
for Jimmy's breakfast

Anchored half way to Pickles Reef
I hooked on to a Monster of the Deep

He stayed on an hour and a half
Hardly moved

Would take 10 feet of line out
Then I'd get it back again

What he was no one will ever know!
Back to Larooco thoroughly exhausted

Captain Rodney Albury with neighborhood boys on the Tavernier dock years later. Albury reported that when the Larooco *blew an engine near Shark River, FDR wrote him a note: "Dear Captain Albury, come save all our lives."*[9]

Saturday, March 28

A bad blow
and rain in the night
Under way at 1 o'clock

Ran well against strong head wind
At 4:20 anchored just beyond
Jewfish Creek Drawbridge

After supper Jimmy and I rowed around
near and through the bridge
Got a big Mangrove Snapper
a big Jack and five Ladyfish
the latter great fun as they jump
and one nearly came in the boat

While we were gone Monty hooked
a 7½ foot shovel-nose shark

He and LeRoy had a hard time
before they got it in close
Shot it with my revolver

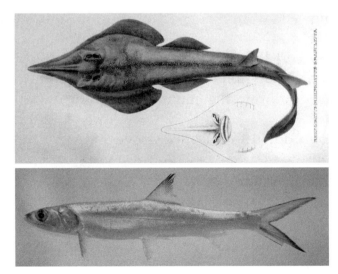

Shovel-nose Shark and Ladyfish

Sunday, March 29

James and Monty fished after breakfast and we got under way at 11:30 and ran straight through to Bear's Cut just below Miami. It has turned much colder.

Monday, March 30

Left Bear's Cut
after James had a cold swim

Docked opposite Royal Palm
James went ashore for mail

Mrs. Morris and I
packed up with LeRoy

Tuesday, March 31

Miami
Packing
Hair cut in morning

James and I went to Fort Lauderdale
Made arrangement at Pilkington's Yacht Basin
to take care of Larooco during the summer

After our return went down to Coconut Grove
Spent 1½ hours with
Mr. and Mrs. William Jennings Bryan

Wednesday, April 1

Placed Larooco out of commission at 6 p.m.
and took train for Warm Springs, Georgia

Here ends a very delightful
2nd Cruise
of the Good Ship "Larooco."

For their winter retreat, the Bryans built a palatial Mediterranean-style villa on Biscayne Bay, a far cry from FDR's houseboat. Bryan was there to promote the delights of southern palm trees, beaches, and sunshine to prospective buyers of real estate.

1926

The months after FDR left the Larooco *in the spring of 1925 were busy ones. In Georgia, he wrote editorials for the* Macon Telegraph *to help out the newspaper's editor, Tom Loyless, principal owner of the Warm Springs spa, financially backed by George Foster Peabody, a good friend of FDR's who first introduced him to Warm Springs. He also headed a campaign to raise ten million dollars for the completion of New York City's Cathedral of St. John the Divine, and was elected chairman of the Taconic State Park Commission, with jurisdiction over New York parks east of the Hudson River. Although his forays into the public world continued, his big political push was on hold. His primary focus remained on his legs.*

On April 10, 1925, nine days after FDR boarded the train for Warm Springs, F. Scott Fitzgerald published The Great Gatsby, *and on May 14, Virginia Woolf's* Mrs. Dalloway *appeared. Neither seemed likely to be on the next* Larooco *reading list.*

On July 8, the New York Times *carried the headline "JEWS TO AID LEGION DRIVE." As chairman of the American Legion Endowment Fund, FDR met with prominent Jews in his office at 55 Liberty Street in Manhattan as part of an effort to raise money to help World War I veterans. Meanwhile, rumors were circulating that Governor Al Smith and Senator Jimmy Walker wanted FDR to become head of the New York Police Department, although, as the* New York Times *reported, "It is not regarded likely that he [Walker] would ask Mr. Roosevelt to take up the arduous work such an appointment would involve, nor is it regarded likely that the present condition of his health would permit Mr. Roosevelt to consider such an offer. Mr. Roosevelt is away from the city undergoing treatment which his friends hope in time will restore him to perfect physical condition."*

In Tennessee, the Scopes trial was underway, with famed lawyer Clarence Darrow (left) defending John Scopes, who was accused of teaching evolution in violation of a new Tennessee law banning the theories of Charles Darwin. FDR's former colleague William Jennings Bryan (right) was the prosecutor, and Scopes was found guilty on July 21. Five days later, Bryan died in his sleep.

On July 18, the first volume of Adolf Hitler's Mein Kampf *was published. Three days later, on his twenty-sixth birthday, Ernest Hemingway began to write his first novel,* The Sun Also Rises, *which was published in October 1926.*

On August 17, Charlie Chaplin's Gold Rush *was released. A month later, Frida Kahlo, eighteen years old and a polio survivor, was in a bus accident and sustained serious injuries that propelled her to quit the study of medicine and take up painting.*

On January 1, 1926, the Roosevelts and friends celebrated the completion of Stone Cottage on the Fall Kill with a New Year's dinner in the brand-new living room. The dinner table was thrown together with lumber on sawhorses, and they all sat on small kegs. In her enthusiasm, Eleanor embroidered the linens for the new house with the initials E M N, for Eleanor, Marion, and Nancy. At the end of the month, FDR turned forty-four, and three days later he and Eleanor arrived on the Larooco.

Here begins the 3rd Cruise
of the Good Ship "Larooco"

After Larooco went out of commission last April 1 Capt. and Mrs. Morris took up to Fort Lauderdale to Capt. Pilkington's Yacht Basin about four miles up the River. Capt. and Mrs. Morris continued to live onboard during the summer and autumn. Twice boats near her in the yard caught fire but she came through safely. A new engine was put in the dory but little else was done except the usual painting and overhauling before commissioning. The bowsprit, broken off last year, was left off entirely, thereby greatly improving her looks. John Entwistle, my chauffeur, arrived Saturday Jan. 30 and Capt. Charlie on February 1.

Tuesday, February 2

Eleanor and I
arrived
at Fort Lauderdale
at noon

three hours late
instead of over a day
as last year

Drove out to
Pilkington Yacht Basin
Capt. Charlie and Mrs. Morris
waiting for us

Larooco went
into commission and
we had lunch

Wednesday, February 3

Intended to start early
but heavy rain blocked plans
Later the tide ran
ebb too strong
to try to go down River
Wrote mail and telegrams

Thursday, February 4

Started—false alarm

Down the River a mile
Both engines went on the blink

Tried to get Miami engine doctor
and failed

Got local man who apparently
in the late p.m. did the necessary

As the boat's engines fail, making movement difficult, Martha Graham founds her dance company, one of the first in the United States. Years later, she will perform at the White House for President Roosevelt.

Friday, February 5

Under way at 9 but current too strong
so sent down for 2 tugs
who finally came and at 1
we were towed down to mouth of River
one tug ahead and other steering astern

A very congested, tortuous River and
will be even more difficult to navigate
when new bridges are finished

Headed for Miami but sundry engine troubles
halted us from time to time and
we made slow progress tying up finally
at the S. end of the well-named Snake Creek
just before reaching Biscayne Bay

Saturday, February 6

Our unlucky spot - vide log of 1924
Got under way at 9 and
promptly ran on a lump in the usual narrow place
Stuck fast

At 10 Eleanor took dory with Capt. Charlie
to try to reach Miami before bank closed
meet Maunsell Crosby and Ethel Douglas Merritt

While the dory was away
I got Larooco off by warping to shore
but then both engines balked

At 4 after a narrow escape from being raked
by a tug and 3 loaded lumber barges
we started and with one engine and the dory towing ahead
got down to 1 mile above Miami upper bridge and anchored

Eleanor came out in the Col. Thompson launch
with Maunsell and Ethel Douglas Merritt and
Henry Breckinridge paid us a short call

On February 6, Ronald Reagan turns fifteen. After he turns twenty-one, he votes for FDR. Throughout his life, Reagan idolizes FDR's personal qualities, though not his policies.

Sunday, February 7

At anchor above Miami all day

Nothing of note

On lookout for possible arrival
of Lady Cynthia and Oswald Mosley

First swimming party

Pate de foie gras No. 1 for supper

Lady Cynthia Mosley and her husband. At the time of their visit to the Larooco, Oswald Mosley has lost his seat as a Conservative in the British Parliament and is preparing to run in the next parliamentary election as a Labour candidate. His views lean increasingly to the left, and he and Cynthia consider themselves Fabian Socialists. Six years later, in 1932, he will found the British Union of Fascists. After Lady Cynthia dies in 1933, he marries Diana Mitford. Their 1936 wedding takes place at the home of Joseph Goebbels, minister of propaganda for Nazi Germany. Adolf Hitler is a guest.

Monday, February 8

Roy Hayes Engine Doctor
came on board early
Pronounced port shaft bent

Took Larooco in tow of dory
with starboard engine running
Passed through bridges up to Vogal's Yard
where we were hauled out

Tuesday, February 9

On the ways at Vogal's Yard all day
New port shaft put in and bottom painted

More shopping and Maunsell motored Ethel Merritt out
to Coral Gables and other swindles

Wednesday, February 10

Came off ways at Miami at 11 a.m.
Got under way at once taking Roy Hayes
along to watch engines

Proceeded from Biscayne Bay and
tied up in Jewfish Creek at 5 p.m.
Sent Hayes back to Miami by train

Thursday, February 11

Fished in vain during morning. Met Missy at Key Largo at 2—only 7 hours late.
Fished again in vain in p.m.

Friday, February 12

In Jewfish Creek
no fish—water murky still

Went through drawbridge
anchored off new dredged channel

The Mosleys wire they cannot get off
till Monday from Palm Beach

At 10 p.m. Eleanor goes to train bound home
Fine mess of crawfish

Saturday, February 13

Left Key Largo at 11
down to Tavernier
anchoring off "Bath Tub"
at Hull's house

All go in for bath
Much appreciated
Crawfish for lunch

Sunday, February 14

Maunsell's birthday
Cake with candles
At anchor off Tavernier

Valentines for all hands
Swim off boat
Caught a few Sailor's-Choice
Trolled in vain

Monday, February 15

Another wonderful day

Went in to Tavernier
Met the Mosleys who
brought us first fishing luck
several small jacks
a grouper and
enough fish for supper

Oswald Mosley, FDR, and Maunsell Crosby.

Tuesday, February 16

Grand trip
to the Reef
in Leonard Low's
new fishboat

Not very rough
but too very
for Missy

At Pickle Reef
Crosby brought in
an 18 lb. barracuda

We then ran north
to Molasses Reef
then back to Pickle
where the fun began

All hands caught fish
including an 18 lb. jack
biggest I ever landed
and a "grumper"
duly photographed by Lady Cynthia

In the evening
the men caught
a 79 lb. hammerhead shark
hooked through the side
and duly shot

Hammerhead Shark

During the day
Roy got a mess of grunts
so that with the crawfish
caught last night
and the arrival of groceries
we shall not starve for a week

Wednesday, February 17

Cloudy and showers in morning
Capt. Morris ashore
to get oranges and grapefruit
from Hull grove
by kindness of Bobby Burns

Lady Cynthia Mosley, FDR, Maunsell Crosby, Frances de Rahm.

Thursday, February 18

Excerpt from an entry by Lady Cynthia Mosley:
"Drank heavily all day resulting in a [word undecipherable] between the Progressive Democrats of U.S. and Socialists of England."

Lady Cynthia and her husband will both stand for Parliament as Labour candidates in 1929, and both will win. Later, when Oswald founds the British Union of Fascists, she supports him. He supports her family by taking her younger sister, Lady Alexandra, as his mistress, and then her stepmother, Grace Curzon.

FDR and Lady Cynthia Mosley's catch.

Friday, February 19

Left trestle 2 anchorage early and ran to Long Key. Took on water, gasoline, mail and telegrams. At 2 it looked like a Norther, so we ran up to Jewfish Bush. Norther in full force with heavy rain and wind at 3:30. The Mosleys simply had to make evening train, so we gave them tea, wrapped them up in slickers and sent them in to Long Key in the dory at 5. When last seen most of Florida Bay was dashing over the good old dory. The Mosleys are a most delightful couple and we shall miss them very much. Dory got back safely with mail. A bad blowy night.

In 1959, Oswald Mosley responded to a London literary agent inquiring about the use of Larooco *photographs on behalf of FDR's son James, who was writing a book about his father, "Mr. Roosvelt [sic] is at liberty to use these photographs in any way he wishes. I have very happy recollections of the voyage with Mr. Roosvelt on his houseboat off Florida. He was a very kind host and we had a very pleasant time. He wrote to us on occasions in subsequent years. But ultimately as you know our political paths diverged very considerably. Those were happy and peaceful days which I recall with pleasure."[10]*

Saturday, February 20

Sent in to Long Key
for Tom Lynch
ice and food

Tom arrived sunburned
Reports rip saw all connected

After lunch we ran down to Stirrup Key
a fine little harbor

Louis Howe, Tom Lynch (a Hyde Park neighbor and friend), FDR, and Eleanor in 1920 on a campaign trip for James Cox, the Democratic presidential candidate. FDR was his vice-presidential running mate.

Sunday, February 21

Tom rip-sawed wood most of night
Maunsell accompanying him on the saxophone
Missy appreciates wood and jazz

Made a fine run past Pigeon Key
Through drawbridge
Anchored in New Found Harbor

Monday, February 22

In morning to Boca Chica where the new bridge cuts off—an old anchorage [two words illegible] Island. Tried for Tarpon in evening but did not raise anything. A nice swim at the point.

Tuesday, February 23

A heavy blow looked imminent
so we ran round to Key West at noon
to gasoline dock for supplies

All went for a drive
over Boca Chica Key
out the new road 15 miles

Land FDR nearly bought at $450 an acre
now selling at over $2000

Wednesday, February 24

A quiet day—Charles S. Peabody and William Hart (the latter of Columbus, Georgia) arrived and we began talking over the possible purchase of Georgia Warm Springs from Geo. Foster Peabody and his nephew. Various repairs to engines, etc. In p.m. went out in launch and caught some small bottom fish.

Thursday, February 25

Went around to Navy Yard
greeted by Capt. and Mrs. Stearnes

Maunsell Crosby left us
much to our regret

Coco Chanel, designer of "the Little Black Dress that all the world will wear," said, "I freed the body," just as FDR hopes to free his through the mineral waters of Warm Springs. The little black dress was featured in Vogue *magazine in October 1926.*

Friday, February 26

At Navy Yard Key West

Tom Lynch left
by evening train

Missy
Hart
Peabody and I
dined with the Stearns

Saturday, February 27

At Navy Yard

Peabody and Hart
left by evening train

Went for another drive in the p.m.

Sunday, February 28

At Navy Yard

Grand motor boat and swimming race
all afternoon
which we saw from Larooco deck

Monday, March 1

John S. Lawrence, joint owner of this good craft arrives on board and the Eastern
Yacht Club burgee replaces the N.Y.Y.C., and the J.S.L. red private signal the blue
of FDR. His first visit in the 3 years we have owned her. Johnny accompanied
by Edwin Farnham (Far-from) Greene of the Pacific Mills. We leave Navy Yard
at 1, steering wheel knuckle breaks as we leave, tie up to destroyer, replace and
at 4 run out of yard and anchor under Mangrove Key at N. of harbor.

Tuesday, March 2

Ran from Mangrove Key
to inside Taylor Key
about 20 miles

More than two decades later, John Lawrence is interviewed by Donald Carmichael, a collector of Roosevelt memorabilia. Lawrence mistakenly reminisces that he made numerous visits to the boat and that they owned the boat for two years. In 1948, Carmichael publishes a pamphlet that includes the interview and letters between FDR and Lawrence.

Starts to blow
Try fishing but
only get a few bottom fish

Wednesday, March 3

At anchor inside Taylor Key
Blowing too hard to move

In p.m. took launch South
to Cudjoe Key
fishing on way
getting a jack and a grouper

Thursday, March 4

Off at 9
Tried to go East outside
Driven back by heavy seas

In p.m. went to Cudjoe Key Station
Telegrams sent and received

Friday, March 5

Started early
Got safely round
to Big Spanish Key Channel

Anchored behind No Name Key
Went in "Shark Factory"
where we got the mended steering knuckle

Then back on board—
the port exhaust manifold cracked
We anchored
Began bumping bottom during the night
Had to move to deeper water

Saturday, March 6

Mended manifold temporarily
Ran to Hog Key
Got groceries and mail

In p.m. went through
to Marathon Harbor
caught jack and grouper

Sunday, March 7

Blowing steadily for five days
Fine bath in shallows

Monday, March 8

In launch all out to reef
Came on to blow hard from N.
Made Long Key
Got mail
At 7 back to ship

Tuesday, March 9

John Lawrence and Greene left for Cuba
Capt. Charlie to Miami
to pay his income tax

Blowing hard—the weather—not Capt. C.

Years later John Lawrence, who had his own physical frailties, described his time on board, "Our general routine was breakfast in Franklin's room, he in bed, followed by a general discussion of what to do that day and often we touched upon national and international affairs. If weather permitted we were lowered in a sling into the launch from which we fished or lay on the sand floats in two feet of water to kick our legs for exercise. After lunch on LAROOCO we always took a nap and then usually moved to a new fishing grounds or a harbor. We looked forward to the big event of the day, one cocktail for each of us and a chowder made from the day's catch."[11]

Wednesday, March 10

Missy and I cleared up
correspondence and files

Went from Channel Key to Long Key
On way back Missy got a 12 lb. Jack

Thursday, March 11

Wind shifted from E. to S.W.
Looked stormy

After lunch
ran past Long Key to Jewfish Bush

Heavy rain
Missy left to take train home

Florida East Coast Railway train crossing Long Key Viaduct.

Friday, March 12

Still blowing
anchored all day at Jewfish Bush

Johnny wires he will not arrive till tomorrow
Capt. Charlie back from Miami

FDR improved his solitary confinement
by exercising on deck
doing accounts
playing solitaire
eating less heavily
and reading Oppenheim

Saturday, March 13

Stayed at Jewfish Bush till the p.m.
when I moved Larooco up to Long Key

½ owner Lawrence turned up
in evening from Havana rather sleepy

Sunday, March 14

John and I trolled
out to reef beyond trestle
all afternoon

Got jacks and a grouper
Back to Long Key
Much discussion

Monday, March 15

William Hart comes from Columbus, Ga.

John left for the North

Hart and I discussed plans for Warm Springs
all day and evening

Earlier FDR had written to Lawrence from Warm Springs, "Here, however, is a question which, since I left Florida, has come somewhat strongly into my mind. The two months in Florida this year and last did me an undoubted amount of good, yet I realize that on a houseboat it is very difficult to get the kind of exercise I need, i.e., swimming in warm water. The sharks make it impossible to play around in deep water for any length of time, and the sand beaches are few and far between, and even on them I get sunlight chiefly, but very little swimming. There is now no question that this Warm Springs pool does my legs more good than anything else. . . . Therefore, from the sole consideration of getting my legs back I must contemplate next winter giving up the Florida trip and coming here instead."[12]

Tuesday, March 16

Elliott arrived early looking rather pale
Hart left at 11 and we got under way
and ran up before lunch to 2 miles N.W. of Bow Leg Key

Elliott and I and the two Capts. and Roy
took the row boat and launch through a cut
then in a N. direction about 3 miles past 3 Keys on right

Got into rowboat and pushed her over mud
to a wonderful deep pool between 3rd and 4th Keys
Pool full of fish of all kinds
and apparently never visited

Got a dozen or more very large red snappers
some up to 5 lbs. and also a very large gag—about 10 lbs.
This pool is a real discovery

Wednesday, March 17

Blowing hard in a.m.
In p.m. Elliott and I went back to our pool
Spent time trying to harpoon whip-rays

Struck one but harpoon pulled out
Got another grouper
So we look forward to more chowder

Thursday, March 18

Sent dory in to Long Key for mail and after lunch we ran up to Tavernier and
anchored off the Hull Cottage. Elliott and I went in for a swim in the Bath Tub
and his "tan" came off after the application of soap!

Friday, March 19

Tavernier. Off early for a day on the reef in Mr. Leonard Low's excellent launch.
An onshore breeze made it a bit choppy and Elliott was about to succumb
when a 12 lb. grouper struck his hook. For a minute it was a grave question as
to whether grouper would come in or breakfast go out. Grouper came in, and
Elliott beat Jimmy's record by retaining his insides. We made a record catch of
groupers, 15 in all and 1 barracuda. Total weight well up to 150 lbs. This was
the best day's grouper fishing I have had.

GROUPER CHOWDER

Cut the eyes and gills out and boil 2 grouper heads in a large stock pot, covering the heads with water. Boil 10 minutes. Cool and separate the meat from the bones and skin, saving all but the bones and skin.

Take a pound of potatoes and cut into 3/4" cubes. Boil in the fish stock until cooked. While the potatoes are cooking, sauté a chopped onion in butter until translucent, add about a pound of grouper fillet cut into 3/4" pieces and add to the fish stock/potato pot, reducing the heat to simmer. Add 1 pound of peeled shrimp, 1 pound of bay scallops, 1 pint of whipping cream, Salt, Pepper, and Old Bay seasoning to taste. Simmer DO NOT BOIL after the grouper and cream are added. It's done in about 10 minutes, when the shrimp are cooked. —from Marlin Magazine

Saturday, March 20

An expedition to Hammonds Point
netted us many dozen grapefruit
from Hull grove
Bobby Burns told us help ourselves
After lunch we ran up to Key Largo
anchored off the new canal

Sunday, March 21

Another grand day—Elliott and the Capt. ashore to see the two excursion trains bearing 2,000 people from Miami to view the "great" Key Largo development. Free ride, free lunch, free motor trip, free lecture, free chance, to agree to buy lot for $2000 worth $20! In p.m. Elliott and I fished to the westward and got 3 ladyfish. A norther looked imminent and we moved Larooco through drawbridge into Jewfish Creek.

Years after he was on the boat, Elliott remembered, "FDR could slide into the water from the small boat that he took from the Larooco to go swimming without help. In shallow water, he could wrestle 2 people at a time. But the best thing of all was that in the shallow water he could stand up unaided."[13]

Elliott Roosevelt.

Monday, March 22

Last night we caught the record fish of all time!

Elliott put out a shark hook baited with half a ladyfish
and about 8 o'clock
we noticed the line was out in the middle of the Creek

It seemed caught on a rock
We got the rowboat and cleared it
Then it ran under Larooco
With Elliott and Roy and John and the Capt. pulling on it
we brought a perfectly enormous Jewfish along side

We could just get his mouth out of the water
and put in 2 other hooks and a gaff
Then Roy shot him 8 times through the head with my revolver

As he seemed fairly dead we hoisted him on the davit
which threatened to snap off at any moment
He was over seven feet long
over 5 feet around and his jaw opened 18 inches
We put him on the hand scale which registers up to 400 lbs.
He weighed more than this as he was ⅔ out of water

We borrowed a Kodak at Key Largo and took many photos

FDR and his prize jewfish.

Tuesday, March 23

Awakened at midnight by a man from Chicago yacht "Adventurer" lying near us, asking for a Doctor. They had gone shark fishing in their launch which caught fire and two of the men were quite badly burned. We gave them some olive oil unguentine.

At 10 a.m. left Jewfish Creek and ran up to Angelfish Creek. Elliott and I and the two Captains caught a large mess of grunts, porgies, pork-fish etc.

Wednesday, March 24

Angelfish Creek

Elliott went sponging with the two Captains
Came back with a dozen nice sheep wools

Angelfish

Parrotfish

After lunch we went fishing again
caught over 30—
large grunts
yellow grunts
porgies
runners
pork-fish
parrot fish
black angelfish
and yellow angelfish!
A fine final day

"Adventurer" anchored close to us
The men with burns are much better

Thursday, March 25

Another glorious day

After breakfast left good old Angelfish Creek
Ran up to Bear Cut near Miami

Elliott ran in to the City with Capt. Bob
while FDR and Roy packed things up

There are 20 large vessels anchored off shore
waiting to get in to Miami

We wonder if the channel is again blocked

Friday, March 26

Spent the day peacefully
near the ole swimming hole
on South side of Bear Cut

Completed packing up things
to be sent to Warm Springs
as Johnny Lawrence and I
have decided to offer
good old Larooco for sale

In the afternoon
we ran into the Miami River
and got ready to leave

Saturday, March 27

At Miami. Completed all final arrangements and said farewell to the good old boat. Elliott and I left on the evening train for Warm Springs.

End of 1926 Cruise

FDR's final log entry.

Postscript

In September 1926 a violent hurricane swept the East Coast of Florida. The Houseboat *Larooco* was laid up at the Pilkington Yacht Basin, about 2 miles up the Fort Lauderdale River. This was near the center of the hurricane area. Most of the yachts were in the big shed, and were destroyed when the river rose and the shed collapsed. *Larooco* was moored outside, along the bank and made fast to two palm trees. As the river rose far above its banks, the two trees were pulled up by the roots, and Larooco started inland on her last voyage. Driven by the hurricane and disregarding river course or channel she finally brought up in a pine forest four miles inland and as the waters receded she settled down comfortably on the pine needles, at least a mile from the nearest water.

As the old strains to the hull were made worse, salvage was impracticable, and she was offered for sale as a hunting lodge—and finally sold for junk in 1927.

So ended a good old craft with a personality. On the whole it was an end to be preferred to that of gasoline barge or lumber lighter.

AFTERWORD

On September 18, 1926, when the historic hurricane hit Florida, hundreds of people died and thousands were injured. Damage to property was enormous, and the *Larooco* was nearly destroyed.

FDR had planned to sell the houseboat anyway because his attention had turned to Warm Springs. As he once said, talking about the fun of sailing, "If you're headed for somewhere and the wind changes, you just change your mind and go somewhere else."[1] One month after he disembarked from the *Larooco* for the last time, he bought the former Victorian spa resort at Warm Springs, where he established a therapeutic haven for polio patients. The *New York Times* took note.

F.D. ROOSEVELT BUYS SPA

Acquires Warm Springs, (Ga.) Property
from G.F. Peabody of New York

WARM SPRINGS, GA., April 26 (AP).
Announcement was made today of the purchase of the Warm Springs resort by Franklin D. Roosevelt of New York, former Assistant Secretary of the Navy, from George Foster Peabody, also of New York. The purchase price was not given.

The Warm Springs property consists of several thousand acres of land, a hotel and several cottages and swimming pools, together with the springs, which flow at the rate of 1,800 gallons per minute. Mr. Roosevelt said he expected to make the property an all-year resort.

119

Doc Roosevelt, as he came to be called, was filled with sympathy for others with polio. Soon his sympathy extended to all those less fortunate than he was. In later years, Louis Howe looked back on FDR's evolution in the aftermath of polio.

You see, he had a thousand interests. You couldn't pin him down. He rode, he swam, he played golf, he sailed, he collected stamps, he politicked, he did about every damn thing under the sun a man could think of doing. Then suddenly there he was flat on his back, with nothing to do but think. He began to read, he began to think, he talked, he gathered people around him—his thoughts expanded, his horizon widened. He began to see the other fellow's point of view. He thought of others who were ill and affected and in want. He dwelt on things which had not bothered him much before. Lying there, he grew bigger day by day.[2]

As FDR's focus was expanding at Warm Springs, Eleanor's focus at Val-Kill was expanding too. She and her cohorts built a larger building next to Stone Cottage for their new business, Val-Kill Industries. They taught local farm workers new skills so they could manufacture Early American furniture, pewter pieces, and weavings to help supplement their dwindling incomes.

FDR continued his close relationships with several women. Whether they were sexual or not is a matter of dispute among historians, but according to one medical report, he displayed no symptoms of *impotentia coeundi* (sexual dysfunction). Missy was always at his side until she had a stroke in 1941. She had been opposed to the sale of the *Larooco*, and soon after the last cruise she suffered a nervous breakdown and was hospitalized. But she returned to work a few months later and continued her role as hostess in Warm Springs.

In 1926, when FDR published *Whither Bound*, a lecture to prep school students at the Milton Academy to mark the establishment of an Alumni War Memorial Foundation, he wrote to Lucy Mercer, "I dedicate this little work, my first, to you."[3] When FDR died nineteen years later, Lucy was with him.

At the same time, Eleanor was becoming a significant public figure independent of Franklin. She blossomed privately, too, delighting in the company of Nancy, Marion, and others in their crowd. A few years later, she became a close companion of her handsome bodyguard, Earl Miller, a New York State

Eleanor Roosevelt.

trooper and former prize-winning swimmer and boxer. He taught her how to ride and bought her a horse. He took her target shooting and taught her to use a pistol. Earl became an intimate member of the extended family, eating meals with them, as did Missy.

Soon after the first *Larooco* cruise, FDR promised himself that he wouldn't reenter politics until he could walk without crutches, but he broke that vow in late 1924 when he delivered the presidential nominating speech for Governor Al Smith. His teenage son James walked him to the stage. James later recalled the occasion.

I was afraid and I know he was too. As we walked—struggled, really—down the aisle to the rear of the platform, he leaned heavily on my arm, gripping me so hard it hurt.[4]

The crowd cheered as Roosevelt made his way to the podium. He clutched it with both hands, his face glowing, and tossed his head back to acknowledge the jubilation. FDR was the star shining that night, although Smith lost the nomination. Four years later, Roosevelt fully reentered the fray and was elected governor of New York. The stock market crashed one year later. The Roaring Twenties were over. The Great Depression began. In the midst of it all, in 1932, Franklin Delano Roosevelt, still unable to walk, was elected president of the United States.

FACSIMILE OF THE *LAROOCO* LOG

LOG BOOK
LAROOCO

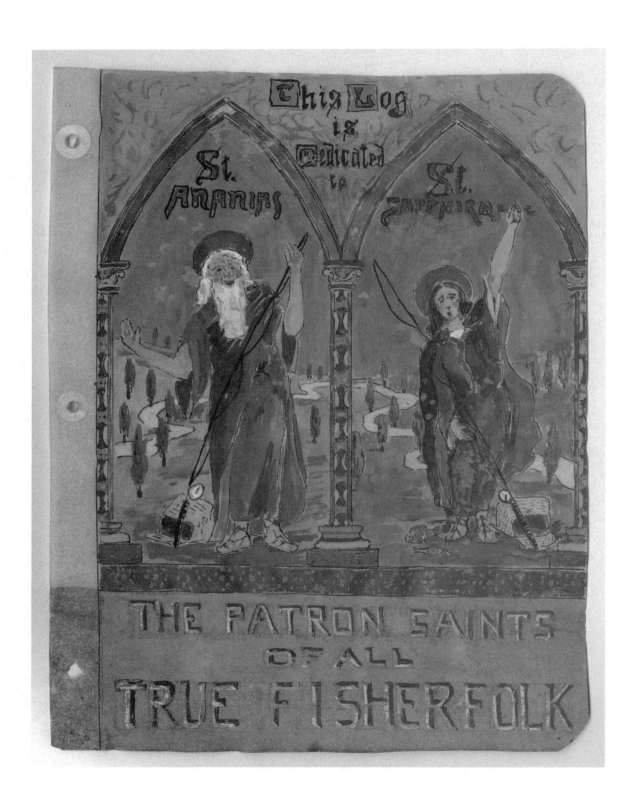

FROM POLITICS TO PAINT. Franklin D. Roosevelt, cruising in Florida, far from the clamor of Washington, touches up the furniture of his houseboat. *Herald-Sun Photo.*

1924 - Anna and Elliott at Miami Beach

132 / FDR on His Houseboat

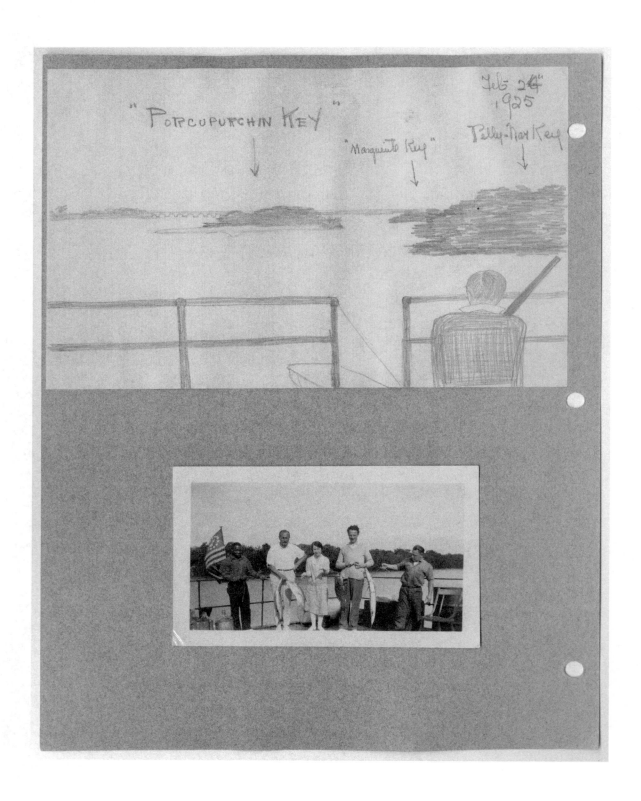

R U L E S

For log-book scribes

1.

This Log Book must be entirely accurate and truthful. In putting down weights and numbers of fish, however, the following tables may be used: Weights.

```
2 oz. make  -  1 log book pound
5 log book pounds made -  "a large fish"
2"large fish" make - "A record day's catch".
```

          Measures.

```
2 inches make - 1 log book foot.
2 log book feet make - "Big as a whale".
Anything above "whale" size may be described
as an "Icthyosaurus".
(Note - In describing fish that got away all these
measures may be doubled - it is also permitted, when
over 30 seconds are required to pull in a fish to
say "After half an hour's hard fighting  - - ".
```

11.

The poetically inclined are warned that LAROCCO does not rhyme with Morocco. Also the combinations "knows I felt" to rhyme with Roosevelt and "Saw hence" to rhyme with Lawrence are not permitted.

111.

Verbatim reports of the private conversations of the chief engineer with his carburetor must be represented only thus -
"x ! ! x ! -- ? ? X ! - - -".

1V.

All references to "community life" must be written in code.

V.

The leaves of this Log are made to be easily removed. All frank opinions as to the character, habits and general personality of one's shipmates written after a 3 days' nor'wester and no fish will be so removed.

Larooco
1924

Sat. Feb. 2.
        At Jacksonville, Florida. F.D.R. went on
board & put Larooco in commission. Sailing-
master Robert S. Morris and Mrs. Morris spent
the day getting provisions, and the trunks etc
were duly unpacked, fishing gear stowed &
Library of the World's Worst Literature placed on
shelves.

Sun. Feb. 3
        Gave all hands opportunity to go to Church. No
Takers. Hence left dock at 11.30 a.m. proceeding down St. John's River, about 18 miles,
thence south into Canal. Very narrow channel
and little water. Most of the way a straight
cut through young pine lands. Moored to
old piling at 5.30 p.m., 2 or 3 miles short
of the Toll Chain. Pondered deeply over interior decorations (of boat—not self)—green or
light blue—or both?

Mon. Feb 4.
Started at 9.30, coming out soon into a marshy
river—strong head wind. Anchored at St. Augustine
at 2.30 p.m. A hard rain in the late afternoon pro-
duced some new leaks in the cabin & in my (port)
stateroom. Got some delicious oysters & whitefish. A.

Tues. Feb. 5.
Shopping by Dora etc in the afternoon. The Captain
found a 23 foot sea-skiff (dory-type) 7 ft. beam,
2 cycle Bridgeport engine. Tried her out in St Augustine
bay for an hour, Then bought her from Mr.
George Washington Corbett for $375.—. At six
Maunsell Crosby came on board, just in from N.Y.
Yesterday when approaching the town we
saw the flags at half mast—President Wilson
died Sunday morning. Our own ensign will
remain at half mast for 30 days.

Wed. Feb. 6.

Got under way at St. Augustine at 9.30 passing south through drawbridge, thence up river into some very narrow places. At noon, just after passing Matanzas Inlet the steering cable slipped & we blew sideways & gracefully on to a sand bar. Tide going out. Larooco soon high & dry & at an angle. M.S.C., M.A.L. & FDR. went fishing in the inlet. Caught one sea trout. M.S.C. identified 33 different species of birds, including a very large flock of black skimmers. Also a flock of Greater Snow Goose. All hands played solitaire. M.A.L. ate too much. At 9 p.m. the incoming tide lifted Larooco clear & Capt. Morris in the darkness & without a searchlight got her into the mouth of the canal where we tied up for the night. Fine piece of piloting.

Thurs. Feb.7.

Under weigh at 9.30. Ran five miles & were stopped by a slip in the canal. Freight boat aground. Seven other boats, including 2 other houseboats & Larooco soon tied up. The N.W. wind had driven the water out. Dredge working towards the shoal place. Will reach there in two months at present rate of progress. M.A.L. & FDR in launch fishing in p.m. No luck. M.S.C. & Geo. Dyer the engineer hunting towards the beach. Additional birds identified. Painted 3/4 of a chair — booful blue.

Fri. Feb.8.

Wind still N.W. So no chance of release today. All three days have been brilliant sunshine but chilly air & really cold at night. At 10 M.S.C. & Capt. Morris went south about 10 miles to the Toll bridge & store & came back (from "Ocean City") with a live Turkey, a big fish (bought) & other grub. The houseboat "Priscilla" astern of us, a Mr. & Mrs. Devore of Detroit & children almost starving. They also shopped & all is well. The "Lounger III" belonging to some upper crust persons tried to be smart & buck by pushing by us. Stuck in sand. Bent propeller. Just deserts. She

Sat. Feb. 9th

Very cold night. Waited for the N.E. wind to blow some more water into the ridiculous canal. At 4 p.m. the freight boat got through, then the Lounger, then "Larooco" and the 2nd boat back of us stuck — we were lucky to get ahead, but in a few minutes the post ——— hit a rock & beat. Tied up at the Toll Bridge 5 miles South.

Sun. Feb. 10th

A little warmer — Passed into the Halifax River, reached Ormonde Bridge at noon — Drew out of order! M.S.C. & M.A.L. to see the famous beach — Through the Draw at last at 4.30. Anchored off Daytona at dark. M.S.C. ashore for telegrams & brought back sad news of death of M.A.L.'s father. Arranged for Train berth etc.

Mon. Feb. 11.

Our party broken up by M.A.L.'s departure for Boston at 7 a.m. Hauled out Larooco at Mathews ships yard. Removed shaft, had it straightened, put back — afloat again at 4.30 Proceeded through bridges to S. of Daytona — anchored for night. Clutch of port engine on the blink. One thing after another.

Tues. Feb. 12.

An uneventful day — Engines have apparently recovered from what sounded like pneumonia. We left Daytona at 9, & kept on South till we stuck in the mud just before reaching the "Haul Over". Anchored for the night. Much playing of solitaire & Parchesi.

Wed. Feb. 13

Off at 8.30. Stopped at the Haul Over for a chicken & some very superior eggs. Came into the broad expanse of Indian River & kept on till 5.30 p.m., a fine days run of 48 nautical miles. Engines working OK.

Thurs. Feb. 14

Yesterday Maunsell took a bath. Reason clothed in mystery. Now it develops that today is his Birthday. Having no other gift I took, a bath also, in his honor. It is a heavenly warm day, shirtsleeve weather for the first time. We painted two dining room chairs blue & liked it & will do the others. Proceeded ever southward. Anchored off Fort Pierce at 6 p.m. & had cake & some flowers for the Birthday dinner. This Indian River is a wonderful body of water, stretching N. & S. for miles & separated by a narrow stretch of beach from the ocean. It is however very shallow almost everywhere.

Feb. Feb 15.

M.S.C. & Mrs. Morris went shopping at Ft. Pierce & we took on more gasoline. Left at ten & it is a wonderful hot day — we are getting to the nearest point to the Gulf Stream. At 3, while passing through Peck Lake we ran aground & stuck aft. Engines would not move her. Channel 50 feet wide. We got our hawser to a mangrove Tree & by the united efforts of the engines & Mac in the motor boat & the Capt & Mansell & Rowe on the windlass she came off in an hour. Passed through the lovely winding Lower Jupiter Narrows into Hobe Sound where we anchored for the night off the Olympia Beach Club.

Sat. Feb. 16.

Left Olympia of the Very Mortals at 9.30, & took our time, going aground two or three times, finally reaching Palm Beach at 4. M.S.C. ashore for mail & papers. I spent several hours trying to find out why the world continues to move on in our absence.

Sun. Feb. 17

In the morning M.S.C. & I went ashore & motored all over Palm Beach for an hour; not having been here since 1904 I found the growth of mushroom millionaires houses luxuriant. The women we saw went well with the place — & we desired to meet them no more than we wished to remain in the harbor even, an hour more than necessary. Up anchor at 1 &

with starboard engine running well & port engine
coughing spasmodically, we got down to the
south end of Lake Worth & anchored for the
night.

Mon. Feb. 18

During the night we dragged & all hands were
called to get her under way & back into the
channel. Started through canal at 9. Very bad
as there are many boulders along it & in it.
Port engine very sick — too sick to be moved most
of the time, so we had Mack ahead towing
us in the launch. Tied up in canal just
above Hillsborough Inlet.

Tues. Feb. 19.

Maxwell to date has seen 98 different varieties
of birds. He had a walk ashore last evening
& added 8 species. We ran aground six times
today — Very bad water. At one place just below
New River Inlet the yacht captains accuse the local
Fort Lauderdale people with dumping rocks into
the channel to make repairs necessary &
bring trade! Painted chairs most of the p.m.
We had to wait just below the inlet for 3
hours till the tide rose.

Wed. Feb. 20.

Started at 7 — All went well till we got to
Dumfoundling Lake — well named. Ran aground
at S. end trying to let another yacht by.
Port engine in locomotor condition again. Just
as we got to N. end of Biscayne Bay we blew into
the bushes — broke two windows — a barge came
along & towed us four miles, part way down the
Bay. Anchored. M.S.C. went on to Miami for
food & telegrams. They had just left when we
had an hour of bad rain squalls. At 4 started
up again. Ran through the bridges successfully, both
engines working, went up the Miami River & moored
to dock on right bank just short of the first
bridge. Miami or Bust. Bust lost.
So ends the a three month's voyage.

ɩi Herald

MORNING, FEBRUARY 24, 1924.   SEVENTY-TWO PAGES TODAY

1920 CANDIDATE FOR VICE PRESIDENCY COMES HERE TO PLAY

Franklin D. Roosevelt, former assistant secretary of the navy and who was democratic candidate for the vice presidency in 1920, is just folks, too, and when he plays he plays the way just folks would play. He caught by the photographer yesterday in an unguarded moment aboard his yacht Larooca, where he had spread tarpaulin on the deck and was busy plying brush, re-furbishing some of the furniture. Mr. Roosevelt has just returned from a fishing cruise in the Florida keys. He is making his headquarters in Miami. Photograph by The Miami Herald.

144 / FDR on His Houseboat

Thurs. Feb. 21ᵗʰ

Miami — M.S.C. shopped, opened bank account for me etc in the morning. Engine doctor began diagnosis. In p.m. with M.S.C. motored to Miami Beach, called on the James M. Cox's who were out, went to Cocoanut Grove, called on Wm. J. Bryan who came out to the car & we had a nice talk.

Fri. Feb. 22

Miami — Engine doctor still at work. His patient may respond to heroic treatment. M.S.C. Mac, Robin & I left at 10.30 in the launch, ran down to Bear Cut, trolled for an hour or so, got one small mackerel, went ashore at the point on South side where we spent those delightful days last year, had lunch, & Maxwell & I took off all raiment & swam & lay on the sand for two hours. Got back to Larooco at 5ᵗʰ.

Sat. Feb. 23

Port engine still being worked over. M.L.L. arrived at 1. Much hard work making the boat spick & span. Grand tea party in p.m. Gov. & Mrs. Cox, Tim Ansberry, Ed. N. Hurley, Col. & Mrs. Van Tassel. They staid till after seven. M.L.L. poured Tea, & M.S.C. mixed "Larooco drinks".

Sun. Feb. 24

We all, including Capt. & Mrs. Morris went down to Bear Cut in the morning in the launch. Fished in vain, landed at beach on South side, had lunch & then a grand swimming party, followed by sun bath. Home at 3, a final purchase, Hutch & M.S.C. left for home at 10 p.m. He saw 99 different bird species on the trip — We shall miss him much.

Mon. Feb. 25.

M.L.L. & Mrs. Morris ashore shopping. In the p.m. a drive to Miami Beach, to call on J.C. Penny etc.

Tues. Feb. 26.

Tied up at dock all day because of engine repairs — Too much wind to go down Biscayne Bay anyway.

Wed. Feb. 27.

Left Miami at 10 & went down the Bay & anchored inside Pumpkin Key, close to the Mouth of Angel Fish Creek. M.A.L. experienced the first pangs of Mal de Mer as it blew hard on the way down, from the West & gave us a good roll. — In late p.m. tied up inside Creek.

Thurs. Feb. 28

Went in launch with Mac and M.A.L. to get mail etc at Key Largo. On way down were greatly delayed by trolling & failing to find N. entrance to Jewfish Creek. Finally started on return trip at 6.30 p.m. It was dark by the time we got out of Jewfish Creek. I tried by the stars for the South entrance of Steamboat Creek — missed it — passing it at least three times within 100 feet in the dark. Gave it up at 9 p.m. Tried to find the channels W. of the Island, found one line of stakes — lost the next — aground badly three or four times, got through at last, made Pumpkin Key by great luck & ran into Angel Fish Creek without even seeing the marker which we must have passed within 50 feet. — Back on board at 11.30 p.m!

Friday Feb. 29 =

Recuperating at Angel Fish after yesterdays adventures. Caught a few small fish —

Sat. March 1.

Went back to Key Largo in the launch, Taking lunch with us this time, caught no fish, but found a lot of mail. Got back in time for one of Mrs. Morris' delightful suppers.

Sun. March 2

A lovely warm lazy day. Fished for angel fish, grunts, etc & got enough for a meal.

Mon. Mar. 3.

Left Angel Fish Creek after breakfast & ran through to Miami in 5½ hours. Tied up again in the River & took on supplies & did shopping.

A.

Tues Mar. 4th

At Miami. Got the sad news that John Lawrence - ½ owner of & partner in this ancient craft cannot come down to join us as he has to go abroad. A few hours later however a wire came from L. Davis saying he is coming soon. Sent many Telegrams & letters & telephoned several people in Miami.

Wed. Mar 5.

A wire from E.R. says Anna probably cannot come but that Elliott will. Just after lunch Miss Eleanor Hennessy, an old friend of M.A.L.'s arrived from Palm Beach for a week on board. At 4.30 we had another tea party on deck, Mr & Mrs William H. Kelly of Syracuse - the Democratic leader, - and Mr. J.C. Penney, the chain store man who has a large farm near Hopewell Junction, Dutchess Co. Much discussion of cows, politics & boy-scouts.

Thurs. Mar 6th.

Left Miami early & ran down the bay to Barnes Sound anchoring about half way between Steamboat & Jewfish Keys. Caught a nice mess of crawfish in the evening. I forgot to mention that Geo. Dyer left us in Miami to go home to Rhode Island. He was not really happy on board & was also I think not well. I do not know that he was inefficient with his engines but he certainly did not keep them clean. Mac (Myles McNichols) has taken over George's work & has from his own account had a good deal of engine experience.

Fri. Mar 7.

Moved into Jewfish Creek. Rain, high wind, & engine trouble. E.H., M.A.L. & F.D.R. fished in the creek & caught various mangrove snappers, grunts etc.. Roan is however the enthusiastic champion with the small fish.

Sat. Mar 8—
    Left Jewfish Creek about 11. Finished our
deck en route, & got down to the mouth of
Tavernier Creek about 4. The Captain went
ashore, got mail & some provisions.
Sun. Mar 9—
    As a blow threatened we moored Larooco
into Tavernier Creek. E.H., M.A.L. & F.D.R.
went through the Creek to the ocean & landed
at the Albury's little dock at Tavernier.
Almost all inhabitants of the settlement are
Albury's — those not so named are at
least close relatives. We swam in the p.m.
Mon. Mar 10—
    It blew too hard to go fishing on the reef,
so we fished in the Creek & went swimming
again at the delightful beach on the
bay side of the settlement.
Tues. Mar 11—
    All hands went reef fishing in Mr. M.R.
Albury's launch. It was pretty rough & we
only got two Cero Mackerel & two Barracuda.
Wed. Mar 12—
    Miss Hennessy left us at noon — very
sad not to be able to wait to meet the
attractions of Davis who comes next Sunday.

Thurs Mar 13— Blowing hard all day —
            Staid in Creek.
Fri.   Mar 14— Ditto — This year has been
considered a very poor one as to weather
down here — a lot of wind, large temperature changes etc.
Sat. Mar 15—
    A grand fishing party in the Albury
launch to the reef. We got nearly 40
Barracuda, Cero Mackerel & Spanish
Mackerel. Mrs. Morris caught several
& the water was smooth. A grand
day.

Sunday Mar. 16:

Livingston Davis arrived at 1 p.m. weighted down with sundry wet & dry goods — he looks like a sick child & is recuperating from shingles, boils, bunions & cold in the head.

A blowy day & we stand in Tavernier Creek. L.D. unpacking fishing gear & I making baits.

Mon. Mar. 17th

Water too cold to swim & wind too high to go to reef — L.D. went to the R.R. bridge to fish & came back minus trousers — to the disgust of the two ladies. Earlier he had exercised on the top deck à la nature. Why do people who must take off their clothes go anywhere where the other sex is present? Capt. Morris remarked quietly that some men get shot for less.

Tues. Mar. 18 —

To the reef with L.D in Mr. Albury's launch. At Pickles reef we found a lee from the swell & got all the fishing we wanted. Caught in all — 35 fish — L.D. 17 & F.D.R. 18 — mostly Cero Mackerel & Barracuda — but including 2 Yellows Jack & several Spanish Mackerel. A shark took a mackerel I was bringing in & I played him for several minutes before he went off with my fish, spoon, & wire inside of him. Our day's catch ran well over 250 pounds of fish.

Wed. Mar. 19th

L.D. went off to the stream alone with Albury, gone all day. It was very hot & the mosquitos began, so at noon we moved Larooco out of the creek. M.A.L & F.D.R. went swimming

Thurs Mar. 20 —

After lunch fished with Albury for small grunts & sailors choice off Tavernier Key on the Ocean side. On our return we picked up Mrs. Albury & Marjorie aged 4, to show them the Larooco. When we got to her a heavy storm was rapidly approaching from the West. We tried to get up anchor to enter the creek but in tracking the rowboat was swamped, all her insides were scattered broadcast over the face of the waters — Albury picked most of them up. Then his painter got foul of our port propeller. Hell to pay. Davies got the awning off but had to disrobe to do it as it was raining. We put out the other anchor & tied everything down & trusted to Heaven that she wouldn't blow ashore. Mrs. Albury & the little girl staid on board & they all slept on the cot & big mattress in the living room.

Friday March 21.
Mac ashore in the launch to get the mail etc. He was held up by the tide at the R.R. bridge. It blew a gale all day. He showed up at 6.30 p.m. stopped his engine too soon, couldn't start it, drifted off into the darkness & Capt. Morris rowed downwind & found him aground. They got back safely. All this day we have feared she would drift or the anchor chain go, but she has come through it all right & the wind is dying down this evening.

Sat. March 22.
Wind much moderated. Engines both working. Off early

Sat. April 5 —

L. Davis waved from the train departing for Key
West at 8.30 a.m. He was seen by Mrs. Morris
who shook a towel at him in reply. We had
a quiet morning & after lunch M.A.L., Mrs.
Morris & I went round to the ocean side of
Long Key & had a fine "bath" in shallow
water — sharks playing on shore from us. —
At 5 Mr. Schutt Jr. the manager of the fishing
Camp & Mr. Bow, the Division Engineer of the
Florida East Coast Ry., came on board & we
had a pleasant hour. In the evening word
came from Mr. M.R. Albury that he or his
brother would come down in their launch
from Tavernier tomorrow.

Sunday April 6.

A quiet morning answering lots of mail
& exercising with canes & crutches. In
the p.m. M.A.L & I went up & down the
trestle for 2 hours in the launch with Capt.
Morris & had a very exciting time. At
the start I hooked a tarpon on a spoon
on my light rod & reel with no brakes
on it. He jumped twice at the start,
took out two hundred feet of line, burned
a bad blister on my thumb but was
still on. I got him in a little, he jumped
again, ran out again & I stopped him by
letting the handle of the little reel bump
past my palm. He was on for 8 minutes
& then the hook pulled out! He looked like a
fish of about 30 pounds.

That was only the start — In a few minutes
I landed a fine kingfish, about 12 pounds,
then M.A.L got a grouper. Next a very big
7 lb. snapper — Then we ended up with
two jacks, another big grouper, another
snapper & two Spanish Mackerel.

At 8 p.m., after dark, the Albury
launch turned up in a fairly rough sea,
with M.R. Albury' brother. Capt. Morris

was wondering why he did not come aboard more quickly, "heard a squawk", asked what that was & Albury answered "Its jut my wife & baby"! So here is the whole family — wife 17 years old & baby 16 months. They are about to go to bed in the guest stateroom.

Mon. April 7.

It blew hard all morning. M.L.d. went ashore to pay the bill at the fishing camp. At 2.30 we got under way as the wind seemed decreasing & with starboard engine running fitfully & the Albury launch lashed to port side — the little motor boat pushing astern we ambled along about 15 miles to near McGinty Key & anchored for the night. Mrs. Albury Jr. & Baby left at Long Key & took train.

Tues. April 8.

A heavenly day. Under way at 8, and anchored off Tavernier — land side at 10 — We had a grand swim while the Capt. & young Albury went ashore — Mr. M. Albury the storekeeper came over to the beach & we had a long talk about the possibility of his starting a gas, water & yacht supply here at Tavernier. At 1.30 Mr. R. Albury came on board with his wife & Marjorie, a grand chance to go free to Miami! They were given the guest stateroom! We started & kept on going without a hitch, through Jewfish Creek bridge & anchored for the night in Barnes Sound.

Wed. April 9.

At 7.30 M.L.d. & Mrs. Minis went to Key Largo to see if any telegrams were there & to tip the Telegraph man Mr. Barcus who has been very kind. We got under way at 10 & had a splendid run with the wind aft. Starboard engine running well & the Albury launch pushing on the port side. Just before we got to the Stilted channel two miles S. of Miami the launch engine went wrong & we anchored for the night.

THOSE LAROO BLUES.

The "Blue Laroo" had a doughty crew
When she sailed for My-am-eye.
Her mast was tall, but her draught was small,
Though her cargo was gin and rye.

For day upon day she at anchor lay
Awaiting a favoring breeze,
Then she skidded along as gay as a song,
Her engines humming like bees.

                                        /t
She stopped at each port with backfire and snor
While they hauled her out to caulk 'er,
Then her engineer got her out o' gear
And never failed to balk 'er.

She would run O.K. across lake and bay
Till the channel grew precarious,   /bank
Then the damned old crank would head for the
In original ways and various.

"Clang, clang, reverse!" and her crew would curse,
The clutch in the gears engaging,
Then in circles wide she'd begin to slide
While the captain stood there raging.

On a bar she'd glide with an ebbing tide
While with hook and oar we'd struggle.   /creak
Then the tide dropped slack and she'd creak and
And down in the sand she'd snuggle.

So, filled with rancor, we'd tow out her anchor,
And drop it in deep water;
Then hand over hand, we'd pull off the sand
And inch by inch we fought 'er.

At the very next turn, we smelt her burn,
For her "mag" had gone to smash,
So she veered once more and shot for shore
And her windows went with a crash.

2.

Oh, day after day, in the self-same way,
She turned and she swerved and she blew.   /slip
There was never ~~aever~~ a ship that could spin and
Like the Beautiful"Blue Laroo."

But grim despair could conquer ne'er
And slowly we reached our goal.
As we gazed with joy, crying "Land,ahoy!"
We struck on a final shoal.

We hired a toward solemn and slow
She started towards port,
Then we cast her free and she went, by Gee!
Just like she'd always ought.

Oh, I'd like to sail on the back of a whale
Or ride on a dangerous gnu,
But never again will I go amain
On the Beautiful "Blue Laroo."

    (With profuse apologies to everybody
concerned.)   M?S.C.

From Mannell hooly 8
F.D.R.   Mar. 1
*   '924*

To
M. S. Crosby

J.S.L.
F.D.R.

Companionable Ornithologist.   "LAROOCO"

Oh the Blue Laroo is missing you
For you taught her things no boat e'er knew
Of the martin purple and heron blue,
And the ways and wiles of the things thatflew

So she slipped her cable one day and went
Down Biscayne Bay on a hunt intent,
Her engines were wheezy, her crank shaft bent
And what the captain was saying he meant!

She bumped a marker and grazed a shoal,
And tried to occupy nearly the whole
Of the big wide Bay. She tried to roll -
And the skipper yelled "I've lost control!"

Oh the Blue Laroo went down the Bay
Like a streak of light at the break of day.
The other boats gave her right of way
And manned the rail and yelled "hurray".

The engines just wouldn't reverse at all -
And the speed grew greater in spite of the
                            call
Of the owner and captain - they wouldn't stall -
And the crew began to howl and bawl.

Her speed got up to 20 knots
Then 30, and 40 - and that's a lot.
The scenery passed like blurs and blots.
Her progress was marked by dashes and dots.

They gave up every effort to steer
And clung to the rail as they saw her clear
The water. But they raised a cheer
As she rose in the air without check or fear.

Then off on the farthest horizon rim
They saw a shape in the ether dim -
A huge bird soaring with plumage trim
Dipping to meet each zephyr's whim.

The Blue Laroo rose up to see
This new companion, and to be
It's fellow in the heavens free -
A new bird species ! - Hully gee!

You ask what was this species new,
And rare, and bright and gorgeous too?
Why, what would charm the Blue Laroo
Except the lovely Pink Bazoo?

(FDR)

Facsimile of the *Larooco* Log / 155

Thurs. April 10 –

Started on the last leg of the cruise. Just after we rounded the point to go into the Miami River the steering cable broke but we had enough headway to get to the Royal Palm dock. The good old craft is thus safely moored after many adventures. The engines have of course given all sorts of trouble, in fact they have been the source of every untoward happening but we knew when she started from N.Y. that the engines were old & would give trouble, & only people with bad indigestion, chronic grouch or bad nerves worried when things went a little less smoothly than if we had the engines running right.

Fri. April 11 –

Seeing people about laying up Larooco & putting new engines in her. Also started packing, & putting away linen, china, etc. In the p.m. went in the launch to Bear's Cut in had a fine swim.

Sat. April 12 –

To Bear's Cut again in the launch for a swim. Busy packing & getting ready to go out of commission.

Sun. April 13 –

Capt & Mrs. Morris, M.A.L. & I went to Bear's Cut for a picnic lunch & final swim. At sundown Larooco went out of commission & at 10.30 p.m. ½ owner F.D.R. left for N.Y. Larooco goes to yard tomorrow & will be cared for during summer by Atlantic Boat Works.

So Ends Cruise No. 1.

1925

Larooco

Cruise Number Two

Foreword

During the past summer & autumn Larooco was laid up at Atlantic Boat Yard, Miami, and was re-engined with 2 Regal Motors. Also the steering wheel was shifted from fore cabin to Top deck, & new electric light motor was installed.

The new work seems to be right but the yard took very bad care of the boat. Chairs & various small articles were stolen. New canvas was laid over whole of Top deck. Capt & Mrs. Morris went on board to live the end of November and helped get things in shape for going into commission.

Wed. Feb. 4ᵗʰ 1925

F.D.R. Arrived Miami – Train just 24 hours late, due to floods in Georgia & the washing of the Florida East Coast R.R. Went straight on board & Larooco went into commission. Rest of day spent in unpacking & shopping by Mrs. Morris & M.A.L.

Thurs. Feb 5.

More shopping replacing stolen furniture (at expense of yard) and laying in supplies. In the afternoon the Executive Council of the Am. Fed. of Labor with wives etc., thirty in all, came on board & I had interesting Talk with William Green, the President, & other leaders.

Fri. Feb. 6.

More shopping etc. Bought a new rowboat to replace the one stolen.

Sat. Feb. 7.

After filling up with water & gas, got under weigh at 12.30 & proceeded down Biscayne Bay. Engines working finely. Ran into Angel Fish Creek & tied up to bushes at 5.15 p.m. LeRoy Jones caught the first fish, a mangrove snapper & enough others were caught by him & Monty Snyder to give us a meal tomorrow.

Sun. Feb. 8.

A quiet day in Angel Fish Creek. After lunch M.A.L & I out in launch & caught 2 big angel fish, 3 snappers, 2 grunts and a large turbot.

Mon. Feb. 9

Left Angel Fish Creek at 9.30 had a quick run through Jew Fish Creek etc. getting to Tavernier at 1.15 p.m. F.D.R. steered most of the way. Had a good swim in the afternoon & sent ashore for mail & the Albury's. The Aquarium on top deck – Two wooden Tubs – did not work – the fish were dead in the morning. Probably too many of them in it.

Tues. Feb. 10.

Sent off a lot of mail, & had a swim in the morning. At 12.30 took launch through Creek to the Albury's at Tavernier on the Ocean Side. Saw most of the Tribe. Made arrangements for them to take the black tother, the daughter of "Twooltie", last year's house boat. Just too rough for outside fishing, so we came back. M.A.L. caught 3 Jacks & a big snapper just outside the Railroad culvert.

Wed. Feb. 11.

A violent thunderstorm & very heavy rain at 5. a.m. Too cold to swim today. At 1 went through Creek & out to Conch Reef with young Low, an Albury nephew — Got some fine Barracouta fishing, over a dozen & all large size. F.D.R. landed a 35 pounder with 12 in thread line & a light rod & reel without any brake on it On way back a heavy squall with rain broke on us, we transferred to our launch at the Albury dock & came through the Creek, darkness & rain notwithstanding. Found Larooco near S. mouth of Creek pounding heavily. Came alongside, W.A.L. climbed on board safely, F.D.R. fell on floor of pounding launch & tore some ligaments. Had to be passed in through galley window. Heavy wind & rain all night, but anchors held.

Thursday. Feb. 12
F.D.R.'s leg possibly broken so got under way at 10 & ran till dark, getting within 2 hours of Miami.

Friday - Feb. 13 - Reached Miami 11 a.m.
W.A.L ashore for Doctor, who came on board & diagnosed only Torn - pulled ligaments & strapped leg up. Tried in vain to locate Mansell Crosby but he had evidently left for Tavernier to find us.

Sat. Feb. 14.
At 1 a.m. a shout from Royal Palm Dock announced arrival of Mansell Crosby, who had gone to Tavernier found our message & came back. Slept late. In p.m. had visits from Mort Newhall, & Col. Van Tassell & Mr. Helm the two latter in real estate business here.

Sun. Feb. 15
A quiet day. Got off mail. Doctor Turner came & reported F.D.R.'s knee mending slowly. F.D.R. still in bed.

Mon. Feb. 16 —

Under way at 10.30, & made a fair run getting to Tarpon Basin at 5.30 p.m. Capt Charles Watkins joined before leaving & will pilot us — act as fish guide below Long Key. After dark they got us a fine mess of crawfish & a grouper for chowder.

The Purchase Contest got actively under way.

Tues. Feb. 17.

Left Tarpon Basin at 9 & reached Tavernier at 11. M.S.C. & the Capt went ashore & got mail & some eggs & 2 live chickens. Under way again. E.S.R. got stiff brace on leg & was carried on deck. Arrived Long Key at 4, got more mail & telegram from Tom Lynch saying he arrives Tomorrow.

Wed. Feb. 18.

Went to Long Key dock for gas — which we found was 34¢ though only 26¢ in Miami. Ran down to anchorage inside of Channel Key as it looks like a Norther. Went back in launch for T.L. but he will not come till Tomorrow.

Thurs. Feb. 19. Tom Lynch arrived safely on board about 9.20 a.m. looking pale (see below) Got under way & ran down to Knights Key, an-choring N. of track inside Hog Key. After lunch M.S.C. & T.L. went fishing & brought back a large mess of fish. 2 jacks, 1 grouper — 2 porgies & over 20 grunts.

Fri. Feb. 20. At anchor Hog Key. M.A.L. & T.L. went fishing — 1 jack — and T.L. looks less pale. An enormous mess of crawfish in eve.

Sat. Feb. 21. Back to Long Key after lunch. Got mail & ran down to Channel Key. T.L. no longer pale, is in fact putting anything on face which his friends suggest.

Sunday - Feb. 22. Birthington's Washday.
F. D. de Rham arrived 3 hours late, but
was met by the gents in launch. She caught
her lunch on way back. She also looks pale.
T.L. today is at opposite extreme & somewhat sen-
sitive about it. After lunch all off to Duck
Key & swam in shallow water among the sponges.
Business of washing each other's backs with sea
soap. After grog Missy & Frances rowed over to
"Whileaway" & nearly got more grog, only they
didn't know it was Mert Newhall shaking it
at them. Service on deck in p.o.s. conducted by Capt Hart.

Mon. Feb. 23. Another Washday. All much disturbed in night by M.S.C. who dreamed he was
a pink Bazoo. Ran up to Long Key & took on
water & gas. Before which H. & M.S.C & T.L.
thoroughly explored Hauzel Key which we
have determined to own. They planted three
coconuts near landing, & brought back convol-
vulus minor & other flora. Parchessi Tournament is progressing in favorably of M.A.L.
T.L. has thirdly consented the use of his face
in place of the port running light. It will
save oil. In p.m. took launch around to
E. of Long Key & all swam. T.L. caught a
jack & 1 jumper on return trip, & FWH
nearly got one about 6 inches long.
Swag in midst of glorious sunset which was
almost as poetic in coloring as F & M's
nighties. Colors remained hoisted. Much
complaint. Answer "We're loadin' ice." Roy
issued our nautical reputation.

Tuesday Feb 24"
Panic during night, as we thought the Leviathan was arriving
in a dense fog; we traced the frantic hoots to our Admiral (every one else
having proved an alibi). Under way at 8 bells, passing through the
draw-bridge most of "Pigeon Key" into the Atlantic Ocean at 5 bells (m.m.);
Then on to "New Found Harbor" where we dropped anchor at 4 1/2 bells (a.m.)
Having made the 35" mile run in 6 hrs & 1/4 against wind & tide ————

Feb 24" continued –

There being unsuccessful attempts at fishing en route me more doubly grateful to T.L. for yesterday's Grouper which made an excellent chowder. In fact it inspired our dear Admiral to give a most graphic and amusing account of his political career from the beginning. About 2.55 "Oh Roy!" and shortly after we all started off in row-boat, with gun, to bathe on beach at "Urchin Key", named for the 40,000,000 "orkukurchins" near the shore which rather dampened our ardour; consequently it turned into a sun bathe and exploration of the island. The latter resulted in the capture of "Blue-eyed Bill" and "Red Rudolf", two very ferocious hermit crabs. In the mean time "Missy" and M.C. waded boldly, with gun in hand to "Pelly-can Key". Grog again was enjoyed mid a marvelous mauve, pink and turquoise sun-set, with clouds of Pelicans and 30 (precisely) man-o'-war birds roosting for the night, while M.C. sits by, still in bathing suit, gun in hand! Supper – "That's your butter don't use mine" – "That's my butter don't use yours". And so all the isto to bed –

Ichthyologist	: M. Lett
Conchologist	: F. de R.
Philatelist	: F.D.P.
Topographist	: T.M.L.
Ornithologist	: M.S.C.
Echinodermatist	: "Capt. Charley"

10 p.m.
"Who is winding up the clock?"

Feb 25" Wed.

The Ornithologist on deck at 5 a.m. but the man-o'-wars had flown even before the crack of dawn. About 10 a.m. with rare tact, the ladies allow the troglets to go swimming off "Lonely Key" all by themselves. Much reading and sewing on deck, and the usual game of Ma-Pa-Cheesy. About 3 p.m. Sudden desire of certain members of the "upstairs crew" to investigate "Munson Island". The Admiral was taking a day off to one his knees, so it ended in "Mr. Crobsy" and "Mrs. dear Ham" trawling over to call on the neighbors. Greeted by Mrs. Munson and later joined by Mrs. Quinn and Miss Ellison. F.d.P. had swim & sun-bath, while M.C. continued fishing. Later Munson men appear to administer the hospitalities – F.d.P. after refusing many offers of refreshments is finally tempted by some very wonderful Spanish Claret. However she was brought back safely to the "Larooco" by "Rummy" who is on the wagon. Grog, sup, and porridge
10 p.m. "It isn't every one can wind up a clock with one lung and reel in a fish with the other!"

Thursday February 26ᵗʰ 1925

"Red Rudolph" has escaped: awful thought — where might he not be!! Finally discovered hid'n in the potato box.

Our Admiral ordered the recruits to report at "Rimson Island" for bathing purposes. — It was deep sea bathing for the Keys. The water nearly came up to our arm pits. "Skinny old thing" really felt that she had it over some of the Island inhabitants in comparison. M.C. & "Tummy" ventured to the other side of Island to get "an altogether sun-burn" while the ladies were more sociable and conventional — Upon departing we were again offered much and many varieties of liquid refreshment, but with great strength of character we all refused. Thereby the Admiral was not made jealous; altho' upon our return he would hardly believe the truth.

Had wonderful plans of poling to P.O. at "Ramrod Key" and then do some real fishing of "Sea" and Tarpon; but a sudden rain storm kept us all at boat. Our Admiral then in frivilous mood took to his accounts and had a glorious time planning to cheat the U.S. Government.

     Grog, sup, and Bridge
      ("sad Conchs!")

Friday February 27ᵗʰ

We have "the boys" so well trained now, they only dare talk in whispers before 8 o'cl. Under way and passing "Rimson Roads" at 8:30. Very peaceful and pleasant voyage to "Key West" with wind "abaft the beam". Lay along "Gulf Dock" by noon having rounded the former ramparts & Navy Yards with thrills — Mad dash for mail before lunch. F.D. closed: great gloom.

After lunch the two ladies go a shopping and a marketing accompanied by T. L. who did much buying of magazines and carrying of bundles. Finally a spree at the "Ice Cream Parlor" in form of "Chocolate Malted Egg Milk Shakes", and then a flying dash back to "Larooco" with ice cream for all on board, before it melted.

Formal call from Commandant, Capt. Stearns from the Navy Yard, asking Our Admiral to moor to dock in Navy Yard Basin on the morrow. Grog; hasty supper and Sad farewell to our departing ship-mate Tom Lynch who had to hope the 7:30 train to N.Y. Bridge; and so on to the "Casa Marina" and then to bed. Mah-Jong Visitors — "It's very interesting" says Mr. Morris

Saturday February 28" 1925

About 10 a.m. shore off and moore at Navy Yard Key P. Another visit from the Captain Stearns who makes a date for himself and family to come to tea. After lunch we all get into "lion rected" touring cars + take a run to the end of Key inspecting new road way construction, golf Club and the "Martello Tower" which was very curious and picturesque. Then, M.S. Missy and Jae P. make formal call at Stearns headquarters and escort them back to "barooka" for orange-ade. Then a delicious swim with the Commandants family off the Navy float, Mrs Stearns looking very charming in green bathing suit, being pulled thru the water by young police dog "Willy". Grog, Supper and Bridge. Again to Casa Marina for mail, but in vain.

Sunday March 1" 1925

"Red Rudolpho" is discovered trying to escape by the davit ropes. Missy and Jae P. have swim before breakfast! Jae P. takes sketching trip all alone. Much signing of letters on deck and settling of accounts. M.C and Jae P. off to St Pauls just in time to get enough but not too much of the service. Church large + cool; singing impressive — Back in time for another swim + sun bath before lunch — "where is Roy?" About 2:30 he finally appears with a package. Hasty farewell to Commandant and family, but they are blistering.

Off at about 7 bells (a.m) to "Boca-Chica" Key where we cast anchor about 2 bells later. Nice beach for bathing where Missy + the Admiral besport themselves, while M.C. + Jae P. go a fishing. Later the Admiral gets a Jack and "Missy" 1/2 a one. "Sans blague" the other 1/2 was bitten off by a barracouta; we saw the fight — Glorious Sun set with magenta and mauve clouds — Skitos so thick that it sounds like a young orchestra outside screen door. Bang! bang! bang! Its only Missy killing flies —— Grog — Supper "Grub and Grits" — A little reading aloud, + early to bed.

P.S.
At lunch time marvelous war time narratives of the "old man with a beard" mentor and the "barrage mine nets" in the North Sea.
P.P.SS. Everyone has now read "Gone Native"

Monday March 2d 1925

Leave "Boco-Chica" about 2 bells (m.n.) arriving "Newfound Harbor" shortly after lunching. Very pleasant sail with much play of games on deck, 4 handed "euchre" being the most exciting —— Getting rather windy. M.C. & Jde'P. sail to "Porcupunchin Key" to take "Tea Rudolph" back to his old home. "The norther really comes at last. Much wind and rain and taking down of awning —— Grog, Supper, Bridge The relating of the dream of King George & the Royal Yacht. "Haberdashine around London" etc —

Tuesday March 3d

3 a.m. Great commotion in crews quarters and at anchor. "Captain Charlie" explains "he just started off on the same hawse line to make her ride more easy" ——

8 a.m. Sunny & clear but still rather windy. Prepare for getting off protected beach on Dawson Island but motor dory comes back too late; so only have sun bath on deck. Leave "Newfound Harbor" during lunch and race to Munson's en passant. Great Cattle ared discussion Agreed only on one King. Must not "Hoss Snaggle" the people. Weigh Anchor at Knights Key about 5 p.m. and all go a fishing along the old Tressell channel.

M.C. and M.h.P. walk up to Marathon to arrange about mail and telegrams. Less said about the fish we caught the better; but Sunset was a consolation —— Grog and "King of France" to celebrate "Rummy's" last night. His toast:—
"To the Hardies
    the Frozees
and "Frantares"

Many Spoonerisms were flung, such as "Lace Oibles" "The thick plotters" and "Too good featured and de-natured"; but we decided that "Source of Faiourie" was "not worthy of Mr Crobsy —

Feeding time:— "Toure ont O'range" ——

Wild game of Bridge at which F.P.P. & Jde'P. won the large sum of 60 cents
    "when I say no clubs, I mean—" - - -

Wednesday March 4" 1925

"Innoculation Day" for President Coolidge.
Motor dory out of commission, so "Captain Charley"
and Captain Norris have to row M.C. to the old
trestle dock where he makes "a Marathon on the
trestle with his drunk" ("end quotes") to hop the 11ᵒᵒ
for Miami. The "Blue baroo" is missing you,
our "merry Sun-shine" who, was "the companionable
Ornithologist". After lunch we all fish from
the boat but the result is only the netting of the "catfish" hates. I de P. & M.L.H. go out in row-boat
with our Admiral. He is left in the boat to
fish while the two ladies. In the lee of "I.I. Key"
have a new satisfactory bathe & sun bath —

Troll on the way back with the happy result
of our Admiral hooking two beautiful silver fish.
Captain Charlie called them "bone fish" — well perhaps they were but any way they tasted very good
at dinner time —— Much work on Stamps.

Thursday March 5" 1925

Telegram from Marathon from Crosby saying
that mail was forwarded to "Pigeon Key". So we
brave the wind and sail around to " " through
draw-bridge. Roy & Captain Charley paddle ashore
easily with the wind. " " telephone train to Miami
with broken engine parts of dory to be renewed. Roy has
to row back alone against a high wind and mountain-
ous seas. The fifteen fish consumed by him at supper
last night shifted from port to starboard and back
again, causing skiff to veer badly. Encouraged by
friendly cries from the "baroco", he turned his thoughts
towards tomorrow's dinner, made a mighty effort
and reached ship pale but triumphant; exclaiming
"That's the hardest job I ever had." Great excitement to get
the mail at last. I de P. happy with 13 letters. Then on to "Hog
Key" I de P. & M.L.H. after lunch, row ashore, do a marathon
down R.R. tracks to send telegrams from station at "
Too windy to fish —— In fact quite a "norther" is at
this moment howling outside —

Friday March 6" 1925

"Norther" still raging, but Sun strong enough to warm one if crouching down behind the hatch — Great business of stamp cataloguing and games of "Anna" and Pacheesy. Wind dies down enough to sit on deck a while. "Captain Charlie" suddenly appears off the House-boat "Elaine" which he had piloted down from Long Key. Brought engine parts back from Miami and also mail from Mr. Grobel whom he had met at M. Grocery Co. in the "world's heaviest ulster." Hectic game of "Rum" and reading aloud of choice bits from Marks Train's Auto.

Saturday March 7" 1925

Wind still blowing hard from the N. N. W.
Much collecting of stamps reading + games
One needs "The World's hottest Ulster" on deck.
At 7 bells and 1/2, we weigh anchor and plough through the breezes to Channel Key.
The two captains start off bravely in the outfort dory to Long Key with mail + packages etc. (F & R)

Seasoned mariners as they are they soon returned with things of interest such as mail telegram etc. plus a pale faced descendant of Adam who after having some of the spirit of the ship (poured or injected into him) was identified as Julian Goldman (not the one founded in the Moovies). Then much chatter and noise regarding his inquiry as to what F. D. R. meant by his instructions to catch the morning train from Miami to Long Key.

This subject presented so many angles and the discussion waged so hot that it was unanimously decided by Miss Ily Shutter, James IV, F. D. R. and J. S. who seemed no longer pale faced and as a matter of fact was viking very much like a Red-Skin, that the trip was much too short to permit a full discussion and therefore we should all prepare briefs.

Adjourned for a Rubber of Bridge. Ily Shutter and Jg. against F. D. R. & Thomas IV. Just as

the latter was plainly to be bewildered by and unequal to
run of luck from their unbeatable opponents.
astute and sagacious J.D.R. suddenly realized that
it was time to retire. As the dog—a rythmurist
as J.B. why should he interpret this apparently
hasty decision differently. The night was spent
in a besieged deep sleep at Clewicle Key.

Sunday. March 8th.—
Could we commence the Sabbath in any better way
than to proceed to the station to greet the Heavenly Mrs
Roosevelt was was expected on the "Morning train from
Miami". Again heated discussion as to whom the train
would carry led to a pool that was alleged to be
won by Fly Swatter. At any rate she claimed the progeromey
and was promptly paid. Mrs Roosevelt upon her arrival
at the LaFloreo, vindicated my high opinion of her
by singing the Heavenly duck. I for her sleeping
quarters. Mosquitoes fleas etc. mean nothing to her
so long as the Citrovella holds out.
The lunch was delightful. Bonny to the latest
arrival from the outlying world, and bringing
her charming personality— we listened with untold
interest to charming stories about the Roosevelt children.
and news in general from the North.
The afternoon was spent day J.D.R. & Fly in catching
a fish — with Mrs. J.D.R. Dinner P. K. Johnson
Knitting + Reading.
After the usual evening meal Mr J.D.R. with
Dinner W opened Capt. Charley in Evening Services
which was concluded by all singing
"Onward Christian Soldiers"
A Rubber of Bridge, a hasty retreat by
J.D.R. who with his boyish streak found
it was time to retire or he was about to lose
concluded a perfect Day.   (Julian Coleman)

Sunday, March 8 -
Quiet night - perfectly wonderful day which
we all welcomed after the Norther. Griddle-
cake breakfast. At 10 oclock we set
forth in Larooco for Long Key to get
Mrs. Roosevelt. Heavy book was made
on hour of arrival of 7:02 a.m. train.
FdeR. (most optimistic of the gamblers) set
the hour of 10:30. MAL won - the train
arrived at exactly 10:55. After collecting mail, telegrams etc. + lending our
ears to Mrs. Blossom (who was on Mr.
Talbot's boat) we set off for Knights Key.
Mrs. FdeR. unpacked - pickles, candy, mail
etc. etc. and the serious business of cruising
began. Mrs. FdeR. entertained us at lunch
with stories about the children. Arrived Knights
Key at 4:20 - "The 2 Gents" + FdeR. set off in
row boat and return 1 hour later with one
fish "by fishmer + pati + much bridge.
Again just as J.G. + M.A.L. are gaining one
FdeR "retires"! E.R. sleeps on deck - peacefully!

Monday, March 9.
At 11 oclock all start off in launch with
Capt. Charley + Snyder - deposit FdeR. on
T.T. Key + proceed to troll through trestle, -
no luck - then bottom fishing - "grunt" -
homeward bound + collected FdeR. (who
had achieved her life's ambition) - then lunch
on deck. Off again at 3:30 to fish + swim.
J.G. caught only fish. Grog with pati at
6. After Mrs. deR. am is "packed". Farewell
dinner of delicious fish + then the sad
"good by" to the "Frankest". Bridge at
which J.G. + E.R. were heavy winners - to bed
at 10. Something fell in the night + we
can't decide whether it was Itosella on
J.G. -

Tuesday, March 10.

Off in morning for Boca Chica. Wonderful sail to a little spot of Captain Charley's where we catch about 60 snappers & grunts. J. Goldman the champion. Left right after lunch and dropped anchor about 4:30 at Boca Chica. FDR + JG go in launch to Construction Camp + JG gets a "kitek" in & back with a fellow bootlegger. M.A.L. catches 3 fish standing on ladder in the rays of the setting sun. More bridge at which ER and J.G. are again winners!

Wednesday, March 11.

Tie up at Gulf Refining Dock in Key West about 11 o'clock. ER, JG and M.A.L. ashore for mail, telegrams, tickets, papers, etc. Find the Admiral occupying most of the front page of the papers again with project for rejuvenating democratic party. Much excitement — many pictures of the Admiral with the famous Mr. Goldman. JG and ER spend hours in conversation — subjects ranging from love and marriage to the price of clothes — Mr. Goldman perfectly happy! Early dinner + fond farewells to the departing J.G. who has succeed in buying a compartment by a little gift of $50 to the ticket agent. "I always get what I want!"

Thursday, March 12.

Motor dory being repaired - E.R. + M.A.L. go shopping (afoot) lemonands at Commandant's and return to boat hot and tired. Right after lunch to Navy Yard. Wonderful swim. Commandant and Mrs. Stearns make short call. On deck for colors. Early to bed.

Friday, March 13.

E.R. and M.A.L. have early morning bath and swim, both clinging tightly to float except for three strokes which the daring M.A.L. did from "step to step". Train 5 hours late - J.D.R. has many callers including Capt. Berry of the Coast Guard, Capt. Meyers of the "Patoka" Capt. Stearns and various officers attached to the Yard. The Henry Morgenthau Jr's. arrive at 3:30 tired and hot hollering for a bath. All overboard and have delightful half hour in the water. J.D.R. swimming much better. Capt and Mrs Stearns and one of the "Porters" on board for tea. All hands to bed very early.

Saturday, March 14th.

Still too windy to sail. Mrs. Morgenthau + E.R. drive around Key West with Mrs. Stearns. H.M. + J.D.R. go fishing in motor Sailor + catch nothing. Very rough. Ladies all lunch at Commandant's house. Delicious lunch - very nice time. H.M. + J.D.R. go with Capt. Stearns for a drive around Key West. drive turns out to be real-estate expedition + ladies wait patiently on board for a swim & finally go in alone at 6 o'clock. Gents turn up at 7 - full of wonderful "deals". Purchases by J.D.R., E.M., H.M. + M.A.L. Peacefully toted! (Shark splashed in the Navy Yard, but the ladies are brave - as always).

Sunday, March 15.

Ladies and H.M. up early and have perfectly delicious swim. Wonderfully peaceful and hot. At 11 J.D.R. H.M. and E.M. and M.A.L. in for another swim. Row boat toured M.A.L. Shark not visible, but fresh in our memories. Louis Howe

arrived only 4 hours late + in time
for lunch. Much conversation. L. H is
finally bathed in the ocean — under
protest — and the ladies have a final
swim. Dinner on deck — 14 turns by
4 of the bunch up and down the
dock! 4 beds arrayed on deck after
violent discussion as to where which
snore would annoy the least! Fairly
quiet overhead—!

Monday, March 16.
        Off at 9 o'clock, but not before we all
have our nice swim. Quite rough
and M. A. L. is very quiet till we
anchor, but everyone else is in the
best of condition. Everyone in
launch at 3 o'clock. H. M. is
champion fisherman — catching 3½
fish (with advice + assistance of
"Little Sunshine". After depositing
Mrs. R + Mrs. M and "Little Sunshine"
the motor boat proceeds for a short
distance and then stops! Combined
efforts of Snyder + H. M. + advice
from the Admiral avail nothing —
it just wont go! Finally H. M. poles
and throws the anchor and we
make real progress. After the real
work is over the row boat attaches
itself to us and we arrive safely
on board the "Blue Laroo". Dinner
below. Parcheesi continued while L. H.
and E. R. play piquet at which E. R is
a big winner. FDR. wins Parcheesi and
then stories are swapped.
All sleep on deck after "Little Sunshine"
finds hot water bag filled with cold
water, a pair of bathing slippers and

a slightly damp sponge in her bed!
"Editor of American - Ug - feeling &
smelling a vegetable - "What is this?"
Storekeeper "Turnip!"
"Good night"

Tuesday, March 17. Lying in the smooth waters off Boca Chica
after yesterdays rough trip some of us think with feeling
that we escaped a similar experience to Sir Joseph Spruce's
travelling companion.

  Sir Joseph Spruce - a noted wag
  Was ill into a strangers bag.
  The Stranger from the upper bunk
  Said "Say - Whats up - thats not your Trunk!"
  "I thought as much said Joseph Spruce
  As he repeated this offence"

The Admiral and H.M. Jr. row over to Boca Chica and go
for a swim while the rest lounge about on deck and spend
most of their time discussing what the first chapter of
the "green Hat" is really about. - Strong South East wind
keeps us from going on toward Marathon. Much festivity
in the evening, due to the fact that it is the 20th Wedding
anniversary of the F.D.R.'s Special green paper table cloth
place cards and refreshments. Moving speech by H.M. Jr and a
presentation to the Hon T.D.R. of a pair of linen panties.
Parchesi game at which the Admiral outdistances us all
while his spouse takes two dinners from "little Sunshine"
H.M. - Sir. C.M. and Little Sunshine to bed on deck armed with
citronella.

Wednesday, March 18 - ~~North~~ South East wind still blowing. All spend
morning on deck while a mechanic from Key West puts the
motor boat in order. While having lunch on deck we hear
a big splash - no its not a shark - merely Monty falling
into the water while working on the motor boat.
Still fishing in the afternoon brings us in a big mess of fish -
The Admiral catching 12.
Heavy gloom at the departure of S.R and Missy. Escorted
to Key West by H.M Jr and S.M Poor little Sunshine has no
berth so prospects are that he will have to sit up all night

Thursday, March 19th Can not leave because South East wind is still blowing. In the afternoon we all went fishing, later H.M.Jr. and E.F.M. found a wonderful deep warm pit, surrounded by shallow water and go ice swimming, while Franklin catches a large mess of fish at bottom fishing. Gets a peculiar species of fish known as the hard-shell or cow fish which prepared according to Captain Charlie's recipe tastes deliciously. In the evening while we are playing Parchesi we hear excellent shrieks on deck from Marty. All go up to see him land a big shark — the yellow shark was such a wicked beast, over 6 ft that H.M.Jr. had to shoot him twice through the brain, before he could be landed.

Friday. March 20. Leave 9 A.M for New Found Harbor. Make good time notwithstanding rough weather. Captain Charlie goes ashore and orders provisions to be sent to Marathon the following morning. Fish in motor boat all afternoon — no luck, Engine of motor boat has completely reformed and is now running beautifully. The Admiral teaches E.F.M Kelvin. His strategy wonderful — no wonderful he was such a good secretary of the Navy. Later on we all play a cut throat game of Parchesi.

Saturday. March 21. Leave at 6.30 A.M. Strong South East wind blowing harder than ever, terribly rough. H.M.Jr and E.F.M do not enjoy their breakfast. Both practise self control on deck Admiral serene as usual. Four hours under way due to strong head winds and clogged gasoline line. Stop for many letters at Pigeon Key, then proceed to Marathon where we all get telegrams. In the afternoon F.D.R and H.M.Jr go for a swim off the Larooco, protected from sharks by Captain Charlie in row-boat. Tell stories, play parcheesi — thus to bed.

Sunday - March 22 - Read and wrote letters all morning. Went fishing in the afternoon in the channel from Knights Key Harbor to the sea. Saw two tarpon rolling. Had a dandy swim at the point jutting out into the sea.

Monday March 23 - Left at one oclock in the afternoon for Channel Key. Had a very good run. In the afternoon F.D.R & H.M.Jr. went up to Long Key for mail and telegram. Saw a dream in a green bathing top, sex female, age (?). In the evening strong north wind came up. We were well protected by Channel Key otherwise might have had trouble. Caught a Jack, a Horse-Eye Jack, a Mackerel, a Cuban Yellow Tail & a Snapper.

Tues. Mar. 24.

Left Channel Key at noon, soon after arrival of James, who came through from Groton. After lunch fished the Trestle & H.M. Jr. got a 12 pound Jack & J.R. a Mackerel. In the p.m. the clouds came up & fearing a Norther we ran up to Jewfish Key anchorage. The H. Morgenthau Jr.'s left at 7 p.m. in the dory & got soaked on their way to Long Key in the dory to take the train. Heavy rain but not much wind.

Wed. Mar. 25

At Jewfish Key, N. of Long Key. James & I fished the Trestle in the morning, went outside & got a mess of bottom fish including a Turbot. Heavy rain in p.m. At 6 Fortuna with R. Talbot, Judge Corrigan, Judge Fred. Kernochan, Dr. Rushmore, Wiley Post, & Gallatin Pell came to anchor near us. A fine poker party in the evening.

Thurs. Mar. 26

Ran back before lunch to Long Key to get last mail & telegrams, & then headed North on the homeward journey, getting into Tavernier Creek at four & tying up to the bushes in the basin right by the Railroad culvert.

Fri. Mar. 27

Jimmy & I left at 9.30 with Rodney Albury in latter's launch, ran out to Conch Reef & started fishing. Sea too much for J.R.'s breakfast. Got 4 mackerel &

a number of big Barracouta, Monty Snyder one of 22 lbs. & I one of 25 lbs. Mine measured 3 ft. 4 inches, not as big as the lb. one. Anchored half way to Pickles Reef — still fished & I hooked on to a Monster of the Deep & stayed on just an hour and a half — He hardly moved, would take out 10 feet of line & then I would get it back again. What he was no one will ever know! Got back & Lauroes at 6.30 thoroughly exhausted.

Saturday, March 28th

A bad blow & rain in the night. Under way at 1 o'clock & ran well against strong head wind, reaching Jewfish Creek drawbridge at 4.20 & anchored just beyond it. After supper J.R. & I rowed around near & through the bridge & got a big Mangrove Snapper a big Jack and five Ladyfish, the latter great fun as they jump many times, & one nearly came into the boat. While we were gone Monty hooked a 7½ foot Shovel Nose shark, pulled the deck & he & LeRoy had a hard time before they got it in close & shot it with my revolver.

Sunday, March 29

J.R. & Monty fished after breakfast & we got under way at 11.30 & ran straight through to Bears Cut just below Miami. It has turned much colder.

Mon. March 30

Left Bears Cut at 10.30 after J.R. had had a cold swim. Docked opposite the Royal Palm & J.R. went where for mail etc. — Stopping etc. in p.m. by James & Mrs. Morris, & I packed up with LeRoy.

Tuesday - March 31st

Miami:- Packing & having hair cuts in morning. At 1 Janance I in Scott Watkins (Capt Charlie's son) car went to Fort Lauderdale & made arrangement at Pilkington's Yacht Basin to take care of Larooco during the summer. After our return we went down to Cocoanut Grove & spent 1½ hours with Mr & Mrs. William Jennings Bryan.

Wednesday April 1st

Placed "Larooco" out of commission at 6 p.m. and took train for Warm Springs, Georgia.

Here ends a very delightful

    2nd Cruise

of the Good Ship "Larooco".

Here begins the

3rd Cruise

of the Good Ship "Larooco"

Forsword

After Larooco went out of commission last April 1.
Capt & Mrs. Morris took up to Fort Lauderdale to Capt.
Pilkington's Yacht Basin about four miles up the
River. Capt & Mrs. Morris continued to live on
board during the summer & autumn. Twice boats
near her in the yard caught fire but she came
through safely. A new engine was put in the
dory but little else was done except the usual
painting & overhauling before commissioning.
The bowsprit, broken off last year was left
off entirely, thereby greatly improving her
looks. John Entwistle, my chauffeur arrived
Sat. Jan. 30 — & Capt Charlie on Feb 1.

Tuesday Feb 2.   Eleanor & I arrived at Fort Lauderdale
at noon, only three hours late instead of over
a day late as last year.   Roy with us. Drove
out to Pilkington Yacht Basin where we found
Mrs. Morris & Capt Charlie waiting us. Larooco
went into commission & we had lunch.   In
p.m. R & I drove into town & did a lot of
laying in of supplies.

Wed. Feb 3.   Intended to start early, but a very
heavy rain blocked plans & later the tide was
also too strong to make the try to go down River.
Wrote & sent off mail & telegrams.

Thurs. Feb 4 — Started false alarm. Got down
the River a mile & both engines went
on the blink. Tried to get Roy Hawes the
engine doctor from Miami. Failed. Got local man
who apparently in the late p.m. did the necessary

Friday Feb 5.

Under way at 9, but current too strong so sent down for 2 tugs who finally came & at 1 we were towed down to mouth of River — one tug ahead & other steering astern. A very congested tortuous River & will be even more difficult to navigate when new bridges are finished. Headed for Miami but sundry engine troubles halted us from time to time & we made slow progress, tying up finally at the S end of the well named Snake Creek just before reaching Biscayne Bay.

Sat. Feb. 6. Our unlucky spot! Vide log of 1924. Got under way at 9 and promptly ran on a lump in the usual narrow place. Stuck fast. At 10 A.& R. took dory with Capt. Charlie & try to reach Miami before bank closed — meet Maxwell Crosby & Ethel Douglas Merritt. While the dory was away I got Larooco off by warping to shore, but then both engines balked. At 4, after a narrow escape from being raked by a tug & 3 loaded lumber barges we started & with one engine & the dory towing ahead got down to 1 mile above Miami's upper bridge & anchored. Eleanor came out in the Col. Thompson launch with M.S.C. & E.D.M. Henry Breckinridge paid us a short call

Sun. Feb. 7. At anchor above Miami all day. Nothing of note. On lookout for possible arrival of Lady Cynthia Mosley & Oswald Mosley. First swimming party by M.S.C. & E.D.M. Patre de foie gras No 1 for supper (with accompaniment).

Mon. Feb. 8 Ray Hayes, Engine Doctor, came on board early & pronounced port shaft prop. lifted. Quick took Larooco in tow of dory, & with starboard engine running, successfully passed through bridges & up to Vaga's Yard where we were hauled out. The ladies & Maxwell do much shopping.

Tues. Feb. 9. On the ways at Vogel's Yard
all day. New port shaft put in & bottom
painted. More shopping - M.S.C. motored
to R.R. out & back & beat tables & other swindles.

Wed. Feb. 10. Came off ways at Miami at 11 a.m.
& got under way at once, taking Ray Hayes along
to watch engines. Rounded down Biscayne
Bay - tied up in Jewfish Creek at 5 p.m.
Sent Hayes back to Miami by 10.30 Train.

Thurs. Feb. 11. Fished in vain during morning.
Met M.A.L. at Key Largo at 1 - only 1 hour
late. Fished again in vain in p.m.

Friday, Feb. 12. In Jewfish Creek. Water very
murky still - no fish. In p.m. went
through drawbridge & anchored off new
dredged channel to Key Largo. The Morleys
were they must get off till Monday from
Palm Beach. At 10 p.m. S.R. got a
train bound home. Fine mess of crawfish.

Sat. Feb. 13 - Left Key Largo at 10 am
down to Tavernier. Mooring off the
"Beth 146" at the Hull's house. In
p.m. all go in for bath in Beth 146.
Much appreciated. Crawfish for lunch.

Sun. Feb. 14 - At anchor off Tavernier. M.A.L.'s
Birthday. Cake with candles & Also Valentines
for all hands. Swim off boat. In p.m.
ran into Tavernier Creek & tied up near R.R.
bridge. Caught a few very small Sailor's
Choice & trolled in vain.

Mon. Feb. 15 - Another wonderful day. Went in to
Tavernier at 2 & met the Morleys, who brought us the
first fishing luck, several small jacks, a grouper
& enough small fish for supper. At 9.30 Miss Marvin
left us to rejoin her family at Fort Myer.

Tues. Feb 16 — Good trip to the Reef in Leonard Low's new fishboat. Not very rough but too very for M.A.L. At Pickle Reef Crosby brought in an 18 lb barracuda — we then run north to Molasses Reef & got two smaller barracuda, then back to Pickle where the fun began. All hands caught fish — including an 18 lb jack, the biggest I have ever landed, and a nice "grouper", which were duly photographed by Lady Cynthia. In the evening the men caught a 79 lb. hammer head shark, hoisted through the viole & duly shot by Mosley. During the day Reny got a mess of grunts, so that with the crawfish caught last night & the arrival of an order of groceries we shall not starve for a week.

Wed. Feb. 17 — Cloudy & showers in morning. Left Morris ashore to get oranges & grapefruit from the Hull from the birthday of Bobby Burns. Sharks & fish were duly photographed. We then left Tavernier Creek and proceeded forth down Florida Bay amid rain squalls & the sport of porpoises which we reached turtle No 2 where we anchored — & bathing party landed on the adjacent coral beach where Crosby triumphed in single-handed combat with a shark which he dispatched with a hard blow upon the head from the oar of the boat — A crawfish breakfast was digested which brought nightfall — & unless we were moved for no for miles en-roth of wreak 2nd in shade of a garrito of fresh turtle.   (Oswald Mosley)

Thurs: Feb 18. Cakes & sausages for breakfast (Sunday) another bathing party. A coan hunt & great turtle feast at 1.30. Three hours fishing in P.M. out the draw bredge resulted in a harvest full of grunts grumpers catfish. Porgie herbert snappers & a par th goose, the last of which hit John's rawed. Drank heavily all day resulting in a coalition between the Progressive Democrats of U.S. & Socialists of England. Red flag nailed to mast & so to bed.

Thurs: cont: Fresh page needed to tell about Crosby's
jazz pyjamas. On second thoughts better not..
We all dined in his bedroom, compelling him
to retire & dining room for same sleep—

(Lady Cynthia Mosley)

Friday - Feb. 19— Left Tavern 2 anchorage early &
ran to Long Key. Took on water, gasoline
mail & telegrams. At 2 it looked like a Norther,
so ran up to Jewfish Bush. Norther in
full force with heavy rain & wind at 3.20. The
Mosleys simply had to make evening train, so
we gave them tea, wrapped them up in slickers
& sent them in to Long Key in the dory at 5
When last seen most of Florida Bay was
dashing over the poor old dory. The Mosleys
are a most delightful couple & we shall miss
them much. Dory got back safely with mail
& bad blowy night.

Sat. Feb. 20— Sent in to Long Key for 1 can
lunch & ice & food. T.M.L. arrived looking
sunburned & reports Rip Saw all connected.
After lunch we ran down to Stirrup Key, a
fine little harbor.

Sun. Feb. 21— Rip Saw working most of night.
T.M.L. sawed a lot of wood, M.S.C. accompany-
ing him on his saxophone with a hole in it.
M.L. appreciates wood & jazz, but has enough
for the Winter. Made a fine run past
Pigeon Key where a large yacht is hard aground,
through draw bridge & to anchor in
New found Harbor, next to Pelican Key.

Mon. Feb. 22nd In morning to Boca Chica where
the new bridge cuts off our old anchorage Perkins
Island. Tried for tarpon in evening but did not
raise anything. A nice swim at the point

Tues Feb 23rd A heavy blow looked imminent so we ran round to Key West at noon & went to the gasoline dock for supplies & sundry repairs. All went for a drive in the p.m. & went out the new road 15 miles over Boca Chica Key. The land I sold nearly bought at $450 an acre is now selling at over $2,000.

Wed. Feb. 24th A quiet day — Charles S. Peabody & William Hart (the latter of Columbus Ga) arrived & we began talking over the possible purchase of Georgia Warm Springs from Geo. Foster Peabody & his nephew. Various repairs to engines, etc. In p.m. went out in launch & caught some small bottom fish.

Thurs. Feb. 25th Went around to Navy Yard & were greeted by Capt. & Mrs. Stearns — Maxwell Crosby left us, much to our regret. Went motoring in p.m. & received callers in p.m. including Col. Robt. M. Thompson & Ad. Brownson who are moored alongside in the "Everglades"

Fri. Feb. 26th At Navy Yard Key West. Tom. Lynch left us by evening train & M.A.L., Hart Peabody & I dined with the Stearns.

Sat. Feb. 27 At Navy Yard. Peabody & Hart left by the evening train. Went for another drive in the p.m.

Sun. Feb. 28th At Navy Yard. Grand motor boat & swimming races all afternoon which we saw from deck of Larooco. Calls from Mr. & Mrs. Meacham, The Porters etc.

Mon. Mar 1. John S. Lawrence, joint owner of this good craft arrives on board & the Eastern Y.C. burgee replaces the N.Y.Y.C. & the U.S.L. red private signal the blue of Fldp. His first visit in the 3 years & 2 hrs owned by

Mon. Mar. 1. cont.

J.S.R. accompanied by Edwin Farnum (Far-from) Somner of the Pacific Mills. We leave Navy yard at 1, steering wheel knuckle breaks as we leave, tie up to destroyer, replace & at 4 run out of yard & anchor under Mangrove Key at N. of harbor.

Tues. Mar. 2.

Ran from Mangrove Key to inside Taylor Key, about 20 miles. Starts to blow. Try fishing but get only a few small bottom fish.

Wed. Mar. 3.

At anchor inside Taylor Key. Blowing too hard outside to move. In p. m. took launch 6 miles south to Cudjoe Key, fishing on way & getting a jack & a grouper.

Thurs. Mar. 4

Off at 9 & tried to go East outside but were driven back by heavy seas. In p. m. went in to Cudjoe Key Station & sent & received telegrams.

Friday March 5.

Started early & got safely round to Big Spanish Key channel & anchored behind No Name Key & went in to the "Shark Factory" where we got the mended steering knuckle at Big Pine Key Station. Then back on board — out to Bahia Honda. The port exhaust manifold cracked & we anchored. During night began bumping bottom & had to move to deeper water.

Sat. March 6. Mended manifold temporarily & ran to Hog Key, close to Marathon. Got groceries & mail. In p. m. went through to Marathon Harbor, caught grouper & jack.

Sun. Mar. 7. Ran up to Channel Key &
in p.m. J.S.L. & Treene went in to Long
Key for mail etc. It has been blowing
steddily for four days. Fine bath in shallows.

Mon. Mar. 8.
All out to reef in launch. On way back
after catching only 1 grouper it came on
to blow hard from N. Made Long Key,
got mail & back to ship at 7 p.m.

Tues. Mar. 9. J.S.L. & Treene left to go to
Cuba — Capt. Charlie Watkins to go to Miami
to pay his income tax. Blowing hard — the
weather — not Capt. C.

Wed. Mar. 10. M.A.L. & I cleared up a lot
of files & correspondence. In p.m. went in
from Channel Key to Long Key & on way back
M.A.L. got a 12 lb. Jack! Still blowing.

Thurs. Mar. 11. Wind shifted from E. to S.W.
Looked stormy. After lunch started & ran
past Long Key to Jew Fish Bush. Heavy Rain.
At 8.30 M.A.L. left to take train home.

Friday, Mar. 12.
Still blowing — Anchored all day at
Jew Fish Bush — J.S.L. wires he will not arrive
till tomorrow. Capt. Charlie came back from
Miami. F.W.R. improved his solitary confinement by much exercising on deck, closing
accounts, playing solitaire, reading Ippendim,
& eating less heartily.

Sat. Mar. 13.
Stayed at Jew Fish Bush till the p.m.
when I moved Larooco up to Long Key. Had
a visit from Mr. Schutt. ½ Owner Lawrence
turned up in evening from Havana, Rather
sleepy but had a very good time!

Sunday, Mar. 14

J. S. L. & I trolled all afternoon, out & cruised beyond trestle 2 etc. Got a couple of jacks & a jewper. Back to Long Key. Much discussion of the cotton industry, New England conference, etc.

Monday, Mar. 15

William Hart came from Columbus Ga. and J. S. L. left for the North at 11 a.m. Hart and I discussed plans for Warm Springs all day & evening. The Fortune arrived & we had a call from Dick Talbot, Casey deRham & Dr. Rushmore. Bill Post too ill to come.
At Long Key all day.

Tues.

Mar. 16

Elliott arrived early, looking rather pale. W. Hart left at 11. & we got under way & ran up before lunch & 2 miles N. W. of Bow Leg Key. Elliott & I & the two capts. & Roy took the row boat & launch through a cut, then in a N. direction about 3 miles past 3 keys on the right. Got into rowboat & pushed her over mud to a wonderful deep pool between 3rd & 4th Keys — Pool full of fish of all kinds & apparently never visited. Got a dozen or more very large red snappers some up to 5 lbs & also a very large gag — about 10 lbs.
This pool is a real discovery.

Wed. Mar. 17

Blowing hard in a.m. so we went back 2 miles through main cut & anchored in behind Bow Leg Key. In p.m. Elliott & I went back to our pool, but spent our time trying to harpoon whip-rays. Struck one but harpoon pulled out after a few minutes. Got another big jewper on the way back, so we look forward to more chowder.

Thurs. Mar. 18
Sent story in to Long Key for mail &
after lunch we ran up to Tavernier & moored
off the Hull cottage. Elliott & I went in for
a swim in the Bath tub & his "tan" came
off under the application of soap!

Friday, Mar. 19th Tavernier
Off early for a day on the reef in
Mr. Leonard Low's excellent launch. An onshore breeze made it a bit choppy & Elliott
was about to succumb when a 12 lb grouper
struck his hook. For a minute it was a
grave question as to whether grouper would
come in or breakfast go out. Grouper
came in, & Elliott beat Jimmy's record by
retaining his insides. We made a record
catch of groupers, 15 in all & 1 barracouta.
Total weight well up to 130 lbs as I got
one of 21 lbs & Capt. Charlie one of 20 lbs.
This was the best day's grouper fishing I
have had.

Sat. Mar. 20th Tavernier
An expedition to Hammond's Point netted
us many dozen delicious grapefruit from
the Hull grove — they are not picked & "Bobby
Burns" told us help ourselves.
After lunch we ran up to Key Largo &
anchored off the new canal to the station.

Sun. Mar. 21st
Another grand day — Elliott & the Capt. ashore
to see the two excursion trains bearing 2,000 people
from Miami to view the "great" Key Largo development. Free ride, free lunch, free realtor
trip, free lecture, free chance to agree to buy
a lot for $2,000 worth $20! In the p.m.
Elliott & I fished to the westward & got 3 Ladyfish — Another hooked in minute & we
moved Larooco through drawbridge into Jew fish creek

Monday, Mar 22.

Last night we caught the record fish of all time! Elliott had put out a shark hook baited with half a ladyfish & about 8 o'clock we noticed the line was out in the middle of the creek. It seemed caught on a rock — we got the rowboat & cleared it. It ran them under Larooco & with E. & Roy & June & the boat pulling on it we finally brought a perfectly enormous jewfish alongside. We could just get his mouth out of water & put in 2 other hooks & a gaff. Then they shot him about 8 times through the head with my revolver. As he seemed to be fairly dead we hoisted him up on the davit which threatened to snap off at any moment. He was over seven feet long over 3 feet around & his jaw opened 18 inches. We put him on the hand scales this morning which registers up to 400 lbs. He weighed more than that, as he was only ½ out of water, so we figure his weight at between 450 and 500 lbs. We borrowed a Kodak & films at Key Largo, & took many photos of him.

After lunch E. & I. trolled & he caught 3 good sized red groupers south of Jew Fish creek using a bait trail.

Tuesday, Mar 23

Awakened at midnight by a man from the Chicago yacht "Adventure" lying near us asking for a doctor. They had gone shark fishing in their launch which caught fire & two of the men were quite badly burned. We gave them some olive oil & unguentine.

At 10 a.m. left Jew Fish creek & ran up to Angel Fish creek. Elliott & I & the two Captains caught a large mess of jacks, groupers, pork-fish etc.

Wed. Mar 24

Angel fish point. Elliott went sponging with the two captains & they came back with a dozen or more nice sheeps-wools. After lunch we went fishing again our last day, & caught over 30 – large grunts, yellow grunts porgies, runners pork fish, parrot fish, black angel fish & yellow angel fish! A fine final day. "Adventurer" came in & anchored close to us & the men with burns are much better.

Thurs. Mar 25

Another glorious day. Left good old Angel fish point after breakfast & ran up to Bear Cut near Miami & after lunch Elliott ran in to the City with Capt. Bob White & Roy spent the afternoon packing things up. There are 18 or 20 large vessels anchored off shore, waiting to get in to Miami. We wonder if the channel is again blocked.

Friday Mar 25

Spent the day peacefully near the "ole swimming hole on the south side of Bear Cut Completed packing up various things to be sent to Warm Springs, as Johnny Lawrence & I have decided to offer good old Larooco for sale, & we have a superfluous quantity of china linen etc. In the afternoon we ran into the Miami River & got things ready to leave.

Sat. Mar 26

At Miami. Completed all final arrangements & said farewell to the good old boat. Elliott & I left on the evening train for Warm Springs.

                    End of 1926 Cruise

                    (Over)

Postscript

In September 1926 a violent hurricane swept the East Coast of Florida. The Houseboat Larooco was laid up at the Pilkington Yacht Basin, about 2 miles up the Fort Lauderdale River. This was near the center of the hurricane area. Most of the yachts were in the big shed, & were destroyed when the river rose and the shed collapsed. "Larooco" was moved outside, along the bank & made fast to two palm trees. As the river rose, far above its banks, the two trees were pulled up by the roots, and Larooco started inland on her last voyage. Driven by the hurricane and disregarding river course or channel she finally brought up in a pine forest four miles inland & as the waters receded she settled down comfortably on the pine needles, at least a mile from the nearest water

As the old strains & the hull were
made worse, salvage was impracticable,
and she was offered for sale as a
hunting lodge — and finally sold for
junk in 1927.

So ended a good old craft with a person-
-ality. On the whole it was an end to
be preferred to that of gasoline barge
or lumber lighter.

Loose Pages and Photos from the Log Notebook

J. S. L.
F. D. R.

2Y

"LAROOCO"

Oh the Blue Laroo is missing you,
For you taught her things no boat e'er knew,
Of the martin purple & heron blue,
And the ways & wiles of the things that flew

—

So she slipped her cable one day & went
Down Biscayne Bay on a hunt intent,
Her engines were wheezy, her crank-shaft bent
And what the captain was saying he meant.

—

She bumped a marker and grazed a shoal,
And tried to occupy nearly the whole
Of the big wide Bay. She tried to roll—
And the skipper yelled "I's lost control!"

194 / FDR on His Houseboat

Oh the Blue Larue went down the Bay,
Left a streak of light at the break of day.
The other boats gave her right of way,
And manned the rail and yelled "hurray."

The engines just wouldn't reverse at all
And the speed grew greater in spite
                                of the call
of the owner & captain — They wouldn't
                                at all —
And the crew began to howl & bawl.

Her speed got up to 20 knots
Then 30 and 40 & that is lots
The scenery passed like blurs & blots
~~For most of her trip~~ —
Her progress was marked by dashes & dots

They gave up every effort & still
hand clung to the rail as they saw her clear
the water. ~~and~~ But they raised a cheer
As she rose in the air without
                              check or fear.

———

Then off on the farthest horizon line
They saw a shape in the ether shine
A huge bird soaring with plumage true
Dipping to meet each zephyr's whim.

The Blue Karoo rose up to ~~greet~~ see
This new companion, and ~~to greet~~
                        follow
~~her~~ Its ~~comrade~~ in the heavens free.
A new bird species! Hully gee!

4.

You ask what *was* this species new
And rare and bright — and gorgeous too?
Why, what would charm the Blue Laroo
~~But~~ Except the lovely Pink Bazoo?

Off "Fly Key"

"Two bells"

J. S. L.
F. D. R.

"LAROOCO"

Good old Ship-mate:—

As me sit crosslegged on the fore hatch, swigging our grog, the admiral's yarns become reminiscent of old Boatsw'n Waddy, who fought with him in the famous naval engagement off Cape Mt. Auburn, in the 4 years war.

First mate Fanny, the female

pirate and the Admiral are much concerned about what the land lubbers in the nations Capitol have done to avert the fate of the good ship Constitution, on which, all three of us took our first cruise. The seamen are all born Democrats, and we fear the gang of Vermont farmers who have usurped the Government, are thinking in

terms of hay rakes and are
oblivious to the Royals and
Stunsails of the ancient
pride of our glorious navy.

Me threatened to maroon
the miserable Republican land
lubbers, unless they careened
the old frigate, overhauled her timbers, and
recoppered her bottom, and we
would appreciate your pulling
your horny fist to paper.

to tell us whether we shall
put the miserable ship
scuttlers ashore on dry
Tortugas Island or not.

Our cruise has been in
unchartered seas. When in
doubt as to the course, we
have steered douse by douse,
half soused. The scuttle-butts
sprang a leak the first day
out, so we have had to
wash in the grog. After several
ablutions we stack off peak-
halyards, flot around in our

little bol, tried him up with
a running bowline and start
the old chantie "Your in
the the navy now"
        Every watch that comes
around me wish Boatsw'n
Daddy were coming over the
rail —
        Your sea loving
and haddy loving Ship-
mates   F.D.P. + F de P

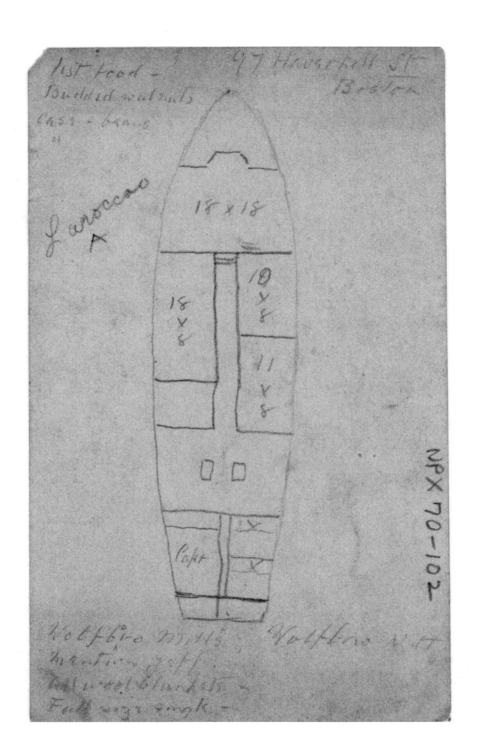

IMAGE CREDITS

Unless noted below, all images are courtesy of the Franklin D. Roosevelt Presidential Library.

The following images are courtesy of the Library of Congress: pages 15, 21, 43, 81 (top left), 43 (top), 51, 54 (bottom), 57, 65, 79 (left), 80, 43 (bottom left), and 109. Images on pages 54 (top) and 79 (left) are from the Carl van Vechten Collection at the Library of Congress. Image on page 87 is from the Bain Collection at the Library of Congress.

Images on pages 39, 45 (left) 45 (right), and 75 (bottom) are courtesy of the National Oceanic and Atmospheric Administration Fisheries Collection (Source: Wikimedia).

Image on page 24: Courtesy of the John F. Kennedy Presidential Library.

Image on page 26: Ephemera. Cox/FDR campaign button (Source: http://kgwrotethis.blogspot.com, Public Domain).

Image on page 70: Ephemera. Julian Goldman matchbook (Source: https://www.pinterest.com, Public Domain).

Image on page 77: Ephemera. Mr. and Mrs. William J. Bryan postcard (Source: https://www.amazon.com, Public Domain).

Images on pages 75 (top) and 93: From Wikimedia Commons.

Image on page 55: Courtesy of the Federal Bureau of Investigation.

Image on page 74: Plagemann Family Photo (Source: Florida Keys History and Discovery Center).

Image on page 79 (right): Harvard Theater Collection, Houghton Library, Harvard University (Source: Wikimedia).

Image on page 81 (top right): National Archives and Records Administration, passport photo (Source: Wikimedia).

Image on page 81 (bottom left): P.D. Jankens (Source: Wikimedia).

Image on page 81 (bottom right): Google Cultural Institute (Source: Wikimedia).

Image on page 82: Rolf Müller, photographer (Source: Wikimedia).

Image on page 84: Soichi Sunami, photographer (Source: Library of Congress).

Image on page 86: Courtesy of the Ronald Reagan Presidential Library (Source: Wikimedia).

Image on page 99: Time/Getty (Source: Wikimedia).

Image on page 104: Florida East Coast Railway train crossing Long Key Viaduct, circa 1912. The Matlack Collection. History Miami, 1978-042-1.

Image on page 108: Karen Chase, photographer.

Image on page 113: Richard Ling, photographer (Source: Wikimedia).

Image on page 112: Stan Shebs, photographer (Source: Wikimedia).

NOTES

Introduction

1. Elliott Roosevelt, ed., *F.D.R.—His Personal Letters (Early Years;1905–1928)*, vol. 2 (New York: Duell, Sloan, and Pearce, 1947), 536.

2. Jean Edward Smith, *FDR* (New York: Random House Reprint, 2008), 203.

3. Donald S. Carmichael, *An Introduction to the Log of the Larooco—Being Chiefly the Correspondence of Franklin D. Roosevelt and John S. Lawrence* (Hyde Park: manuscript if FDR Archives, 1948), 4.

4. Elliott Roosevelt and James Brough, *The Roosevelts of Hyde Park: An Untold Story* (New York: G. P. Putnam's Sons, 1973), 159.

5. Carmichael, *An Introduction*, 7.

6. Ibid., 14.

7. Ibid., 23.

8. Ibid., 20–21.

9. Ibid., 25.

10. Roosevelt and Brough, 196.

11. Hazel Rowley, *Franklin and Eleanor: An Extraordinary Marriage* (New York: Farrar, Straus, and Giroux, 2010), 130.

12. Elliott Roosevelt, *F.D.R.—His Personal Letters (Early Years: 1905–1928)*, vol. 2 (New York: Duell, Sloan, and Pearce, 1947), 582.

13. Kenneth S. Davis, *Invincible Summer: An Intimate Portrait of the Roosevelts, Based on the Recollections of Marion Dickerman* (New York: Atheneum, 1974), 50.

14. Jan Pottker, *Sara and Eleanor* (New York: St. Martins Griffin, 2005), 230.

15. Roosevelt and Brough, 162.

The *Larooco* Log

1. Typed letter from FDR to Maunsell Crosby, stuck in the binder of the original Larooco Log. FDR Archives, Hyde Park, NY.

2. Gertrude Stein, *How Writing Is Written*, vol. 2, ed. Robert Bartlett Haas (Los Angeles: Black Sparrow Press, 1974), 151.

3. Elliott Roosevelt, *F.D.R.—His Personal Letters*, 543.

4. Carmichael, *An Introduction*, 7.

5. Jean Edward Smith, *FDR* (New York: Random House, 2008) (Reprint), 207.

6. Carmichael, *An Introduction*, 32–34.

7. Ibid., 36.

8. Ibid, 41.

9. From exhibit notes by Brad Bertelli from the Florida Keys History Discovery Center, Islamorada, FL.

10. Letter from Oswald Mosley to John Montgomery, University of Birmingham, UK: Cadbury Research Library: Special Collections, Oswald Mosley Letters 1951–1980.

11. Carmichael, *An Introduction*, 5–6.

12. Ibid., 50–51.

13. Roosevelt and Brough, 170.

Afterword

1. Robert F. Cross, *Sailor in the White House: The Seafaring Life of FDR* (Annapolis: Naval Institute Press, 2003), epigraph, n.p.

2. Julie M. Fenster, *FDR's Shadow: Louis Howe, the Force that Shaped Franklin and Eleanor Roosevelt* (New York: Palgrave Macmillan, 2009), 189.

3. Joseph E. Persico, *Franklin and Lucy: Mrs. Rutherfurd and Other Remarkable Women in Roosevelt's Life* (New York: Random House, 2009), 179.

4. James Roosevelt, *My Parents: A Differing View* (Chicago: Playboy Press, 1976), 93.

INDEX

Note: Page numbers in *italics* indicate figures.